O for a Falconer's Voice

MEMORIES OF THE OLD HAWKING CLUB

ROGER UPTON

 The Crowood Press

First published in 1987 by
The Crowood Press
Ramsbury, Marlborough,
Wiltshire SN8 2HE

British Library Cataloguing in Publication Data

Upton, Roger
    O, for a falconer's voice
    1. Falconry
    I. Title
    799.2'32   SK321

    ISBN 1 85223 015 0

*To the memory of three great falconers who did so much
to maintain the sport they loved so well:*

Edward Clough Newcome
The Hon. Gerald Lascelles
Colonel Gilbert Blaine

Typeset by Lee Typesetting, Warminster
Printed in Great Britain
at the University Printing House, Oxford

CONTENTS

Acknowledgements

I would like to thank the following for their help and encouragement:

Lady Black
Dr Umberto Caproni
Stephen Frank
Mr Jack Frost
Kit Garnett
Mrs D. Gladstone
Tony Houston
Robert Jarman (of Debrett's)
The late Norman Knight
Lady Mary Legard
Miss Anastasia Noble
Mark Palmer
Leonard Potter
Ted Roberts
Bill Ruttledge
Lady Stuckley
Mark Upton (photographer)
Peter Upton (artist)
Simon Upton (photographer)
The British Falconers' Club
The Tyron Gallery

Foreword

It has been my privilege to have known Roger Upton for many years and to have read and enjoyed his earlier book, *A Bird in the Hand*, which brought back to me many memories of days spent with some of his celebrated falconers of the past.

I must without a doubt be the oldest surviving member, if not the only surviving member, of the Old Hawking Club – the subject of this book – and I knew Guy Blaine, Ken Palmer, Stanley Allen and Gerry Lascelles, and the professionals, Oxer and Best.

As a boy I enjoyed partridge hawking at Avebury, where my father, Charles Garnett, had the shooting over much of the land between the village and Marlborough. Our hawking lodge there was the house next to the Red Lion. We had some good peregrines and Blaine sometimes joined us with his excellent tiercels from the isle of Lundy.

I was a member of the Old Hawking Club for many years when their headquarters were at Shrewton on the Salisbury Plain. In those days we rode over the downs without seeing a wire fence at all and in the spring hawked rooks and the occasional magpie, which gave much sport and nearly always survived.

These fascinating memoirs of the Old Club must be of great interest to any falconer, sportsman or countryman, and they give me great pleasure in reminding me of those very happy days that seem so long ago.

G. W. G. GARNETT
1987

Introduction

Falconry has always been a sport for individuals, and the skills and arts of its practice have, for long, been passed down from falconer to would-be falconer. It is a sport that has also attracted interest from others who, perhaps, have not the inclination, time or knowledge to pursue the sport with their own hawks, but enjoy watching and being involved in the survival of the old sport. For both of these, hawking clubs have provided opportunity and created continuity.

The history of these clubs, and in particular the Old Hawking Club, which carried the sport into the twentieth century, is of fascinating interest to those of us today who struggle against the odds to attempt to maintain the high standards encouraged and set by such clubs and their members. Equally of interest to the tyro of today is to discover that they too experienced setbacks and failures.

Nearly all of what I have written has, of necessity, been taken from books and diaries, articles and letters, together with some memories of those very few who still live to remember anything of those times. These, their children and grandchildren, I gratefully thank for their help and for the opportunity to share these records and memories with others.

May I quote from the pages of a book written by a member of the Old Hawking Club:

'To those "that are young professors" no less than those "that would learn to profess" I offer this my book, trusting that they may gather something of profit from its pages' (Gilbert Blaine, *Falconry*).

ROGER UPTON

6

1
EARLY
FALCONRY
CLUBS

The Old Hawking Club, founded in 1864, was the last of the great falconry clubs to employ professional falconers and to maintain a large team of club hawks. For sixty-two years the old club kept a first-class establishment of hawks, trained to a variety of quarry, employed and trained falconers and enjoyed sport of a high standard.

The Falconers' Club

The earliest club noted in falconry literature was the Confederate Hawks of Great Britain, more generally known as the Falconers' Club. This club, probably started in 1772 under the presidency of George, third Earl of Orford, grandson of Sir Robert Walpole, was early under the management of Col. Thomas Thornton. For apparently the first time in England, Dutch falconers were employed, Jan Daams being the first to come over from Valkenswaard in 1772, later to be joined by Frank van der Heuvell, Jan Pells, the Bot brothers and Adrian Mollen.

For nine seasons Col. Thornton managed the club and on retiring from office in 1781 was presented with a silver gilt urn suitably designed. Inscribed on the urn was the following:

Colonel Thornton, proposer and manager of the Confederate Hawks, is requested to receive this piece of plate from George, Earl of Orford, together with the united thanks of the members of the Falconers' Club, as a testimony of their esteem and just sense of his assiduity, and of the unparalleled excellence to which, in the course of nine years' management, he has brought them, when, unable to attend them any longer, he made them a present to the Earl of Orford. Barton Mills, 23rd June 1781.

Colonel Thornton taking up a heron hawk.

Members of the Club.

Earl of Orford	Mr Vaughan
Mr Sturt	Mr R. Wilson
Mr Snow	Mr Musters
Mr Smith	Mr Barrington Price
Mr Stevens	Mr Daniel
Earl Ferrers	Hon. Mr Rowley
Hon. Thos. Shirley	Lord Mulgrave
Sir Thos. Tancred	Capt. Grimston
Mr A. Wilkinson	Capt. Yarburgh
Mr B. Wrightson	Earl of Leicester
Mr Drummond	Mr Stanhope
Sir Cornwallis Maude	Mr Leighton
Duke of Ancaster	Mr Francis Barnard
Mr Williamson	Mr Nelthorpe
Mr Baker	Mr Porter
Mr William Baker	Colonel St. Leger
Mr Pierce	Mr Searle
Mr Coke	Mr Parkhurst
Duke of Rutland	Mr Molyneux
Mr Belford	Earl of Surrey

Mr Lascelles Lascelles   Sir William Milner
Mr Parker   Sir John Ramsden
Mr Tyssen   Mr Royds
Mr Molloy   Sir Richard Symonds
Mr Affleck   Earl of Leinster
Mr St. George   Earl of Lincoln
Earl of Eglinton   Marquis of Granby
    Mr Parsons

Chaplain – Mr Edward Parsons

Lord Orford took over the management of the club and maintained sport on a princely scale until his death in 1792. Kites were the principle quarry and both peregrines and gyrfalcons were used, as can be seen from a contemporary advertisement:

Swaffham,
February 5th 1783.

Hawking
Earl of Orford, Manager of this Year.

The gentlemen of the Falconers' Society are hereby acquainted, that the hawks will be in England in the first week in March, and will begin kite and crow hawking immediately on the arrival. The quarters are fixed at Bourn Bridge, Cambridgeshire, forty-eight miles from London, until the first April Meeting, when they will go to Barton Mills and Brandon till the 31st May, when the season will finish.

The hawks to be out every Saturday, Monday, and Wednesday, in each week at ten o'clock, provided the weather is favourable.

Subscribers are desired to pay in their subscriptions, for this season, on or before the 20th March, to Messrs. Coutts and Co., Bankers in the Strand, London.

N.B. The cage consists of thirty-two slight falcons, thirteen German hawks,[1] and seven Iceland falcons.

The red or fork-tailed kite was still relatively common in Lord Orford's time, and especially abundant in districts rich in rabbits, such as those around Alconbury Hill, Huntingdonshire, Eriswell and Brandon in Suffolk, and in parts of Cambridgeshire. Kites, much prone to soaring at great heights, were lured within range of the waiting falconers by the clever use of a live owl. Blome in 1686 wrote:

There is a pretty way for the flying at the Kyte, which affords good diversion; it is thus performed: Get an Owl, and tye a small Fox tail or some such

---

1   The 'German hawks' were probably goshawks.

devise to one of her legs, that she may not give you the Go-by, and being in the Field, the day being warm and clear, you will soon discover a Kyte cooling herself in the Air, then let your Owl fly, and the Kyte will not fail to make near her to gaze upon her, and when the Kyte is descended pretty near her, then let fly your Hawk, and the Kyte perceiving the surprise, doth endeavour to preserve herself by mounting up and winding the most she can. And here the Combat begins, but oft-times none can see when it ends, both mounting out of sight; but in the end the Hawk becomes Victor, and by main strength and courage beats down the Kyte, yet not without many turns and wrenches in the Air to the great pleasure of the Spectators.

Perhaps the best-known account of a flight at kite was written by Colonel Thornton when a large field was out with the Falconers' Club searching for kite near to Elden Gap. At either end of the Elveden, or Elden, Estate, clumps of Scotch firs had been planted beside the Newmarket–Thetford turnpike road which were particularly conspicuous landmarks in a treeless district. To the locals they were known as the Barton Mills and Thetford Gaps, but strangers called either the Elden Gap. The southern, or Barton Mills, gap was the more likely of the two to produce a flight. When a kite was seen high in the air the owl was flown, drawing the kite to a proper distance. The day being fine, three hawks were flown – *Crocus*, a famous peregrine, and with her *Javelin* and *Icelanderkin*, both thought to have been gyrs. A fine flight followed and the enthusiastic company had a good gallop of six miles when the kite was taken. The falconers then tried for a hare with *Sans Quartier*, a famous white gyrfalcon which she killed in about two miles.

After the death of Lord Orford in 1792, the management of the Falconers' Club passed to Captain, later Colonel, Wilson of Didlington, who maintained the club, supported by subscription, until 1838. The hawks were kept at High Ash, close by to Didlington, and as kites became harder to find the club turned to herons for their sport. A heronry had been established at Didlington on the river with open country on all sides suitable for riding over and to there, (towards the end of April) the falconers repaired, having trained the passage falcons at Valkenswaard where they had been trapped. The best time of the year for sport was when the herons had young in the nest and were out foraging for food at some considerable distance from the heronry. The afternoon was the best part of the day, with the hope of intercepting full herons returning with food for their young.

Placing themselves downwind of the heronry, the falconers would

*A falcon belonging to the Confederate Hawks of Great Britain,
painted in 1831 by E. Landseer.*

wait for a returning heron, who would be obliged to fly against the
wind to reach the safety of the heronry. The distance at which a

practised falconer could view a returning heron was remarkable, and, according to the course of the bird, the two falconers would ride out and, when within two or three hundred yards, would slip a cast of hawks. As soon as the heron realised it was being pursued it would disgorge the food from its crop and frog or fish would be seen well out of their natural element, more than one good-sized fish finding its way into a falconer's bag. The heron endeavours to keep above the hawks by spiralling upwards, all the time drifting with the wind, as the falcons ring in huge circles to get above the heron to make a stoop. The three birds often mounted to a great height in the air, the two falcons making frequent stoops until one binds to the heron, the three descending often three or four miles from the start. The falconers would ride hard, regardless of the many rabbit holes, to get up in time to lay hold of the heron, its long neck imprisoned under the falconer's leg, before damage could be done to the falcons. It was the custom at Didlington when the falconers were up in time to take the heron alive to put a brass ring on its leg marked with the date, and then to release it.

A few accounts remain of the day-to-day sport shown by the Falconers' Club. One of them is a fragmentary journal written by Mr J. D. Hoy of Stoke by Nayland.

Wednesday, 15th May [1833]. Left home half-past five, with Goshawk on hand; reached Didlington High Ash about two o'clock. They had lost their best Hawk, called *Bulldog*, the day before. We saw him after the Rooks as we were walking from Nundford. Did not go out: gave some of the Hawks a train-Heron close by.

Thursday, 16th . . . In afternoon had two flights – one a good one – and caught the Heron well in sight after many stoops and turns. The other escaped. One Hawk left and pursued a Missel-Thrush, and the other gave it up after flying about a mile towards the heronry. Day very hot.

Friday, 17th . . . Day very hot and clear. Had one flight, but not a good one. A very good hood-off. Hawks did not behave well. Drove over to Mr. Newcome's in morning, took lunch with him, looked over his gardens and grounds. Saw the Jer Falcon which he had set up for Lord Berners . . . Saw a painting of the Icelander, and a portrait of a nobleman with a Hawk on his hand.

Saturday, 18th . . . Very warm, but not quite so hot as it had been. Went to Cranwich Field, had excellent sport. Two herons came together: they hooded-off *The Old Miller* and another good Hawk. They each took a Heron. *The Miller*, after a good flight, took the Heron. The other Heron mounted by small rings with great rapidity, the Falcon keeping close to him till he got above, and made several stoops, but the Heron kept mounting and got so high that it was scarcely visible, and at times quite lost to sight. The Heron in the end beat him, and the Falcon came down from his dizzy height like an arrow, at two Stock-Doves passing under him, and was taken in by the falconers. Had another flight afterwards, the Hawk with a good deal of work caught the Heron, but let it go on the ground, and afterwards she had an excellent flight with many stoops, but would not catch again. They lured the Hawks after flying a long time . . .

Left home Sunday evening, June 23rd . . . Started Monday morning . . . reached Mundford at one o'clock, and the High Ash a quarter before two. Went down to the Hall with the falconers, and from thence to Cranwich Field. A heavy shower of rain came on; afterwards a fine evening. Many Herons went over: hooded a Rook-Hawk off at a Heron, rather low, as we could not find a Rook, but he would not mount: came prettily at the Pigeon, when he was taken in. Missed two or three chances at Herons during this time. Two Herons shortly after came over together. A fine hood-off, but unluckily the Hawks divided, and each took a Heron. One made up to the Heron and made two good stoops, but neither of the Hawks would fly well singly. He then left his Heron, and was taken in. The other mounted well and made two or three rings and left also, and came down with great velocity at the Pigeon, stooping at it several times. Two Herons again soon made their appearance, and we had a splendid hood-off. *The Old Miller* and the Haggard Jer. The Heron was high, but they mounted very quickly. The Heron soon found that mischief was intended and mounted, screaming. He was a light Heron.[2] The Hawks flew in wide circles and soon outsoared their quarry. Several fine stoops were then made, and one Hawk, making a rapid and lofty stoop, seized the Heron. The other bound to him almost immediately, and they fell within a short distance of me. The Heron was so disabled (his back appeared broken) that we killed him. Several other Herons went over: hooded a Rook-Hawk off at a Heron, rather low, as we the falconers riding to get the windward of them. Lord Berners out, and a tolerable field – Both the Newcomes.

In 1832, Colonel Wilson had inherited the title of Lord Berners and for a further six years was the mainstay of the Falconers' Club although the Duke of Leeds, then still Lord Carmarthen, was nominally head and the young Mr Edward Clough Newcome its most active member. Edward's brother, William Cyril Newcome, the rector of Boothby in Lincolnshire, was a frequent member in the field at the Didlington meets when quite a boy, about thirteen or fourteen years of age, in the late 1820s. Unfortunately, neither boy kept any records of the sport enjoyed but memory gave pen to some interesting notes in Lubbock's *Fauna of Norfolk*:

---

2   A light heron has no food in its crop and therefore flies well and mounts quickly.

Col. Wilson kept the Hawks then at the High Ash, and the falconers lived there also. I can remember old Frank (van de Heuvell), and James and 'Noll' Bots. The meets were, according to the wind, at High Ash, Mundford, Cranwich Barn, Northwold Field, and Methwold Field – Cranwich being far the best. Many a time have I gone to those places with my poor brother, and have spent many an hour waiting for a Heron. Latterly, as the open fields got to be cultivated, the farmers objected to our riding over their corn, and the extent of our ground was lessened . . . I think I can remember the day Hoy mentions. *The Old Miller* was one of a favourite cast; I can't remember the other. *The Miller* was told off to help the Gyr Falcon; probably the Heron was crippled by the Gyr's stoop. I have seen Herons killed dead in the air by Gyr Falcons, but they are a failure in hawking, as they don't stick to their prey, and soon give up. The field out with the Didlington Hawks used to consist of the neighbourhood, Lord Berners and his brother, Col. Peel, Vincent Ayre, Waddington, Caldwell, Tyssen, besides the Duke of Leeds, Mr. Charles Stuart-Wortley, and my brother. Some rather ludicrous scenes occasionally happened. Old Lord Berners was very fond of his bottle of port, and at times came out very late in the evening. One day he met the falconers going home after having fed-up their Hawks. He made them turn back. Herons kept coming, but the vision of his party was rather obscured by the old 'beeswing', and they were not noticed. At last one came so near that they could not help seeing it, and the falconers were obliged to hood off. Luckily the Hawks alighted on the ground and were taken up again. The party went home in the dark not much edified by hawking. Another time an ardent sportsman, but unfortunately short-sighted, when the Hawks were unhooded, got sight of a lapwing which had a nest near, and was mobbing and stooping at a Crow. He rode after the birds exclaiming, 'How beautiful! How grand! What a noble sport!' and probably ended his ecstasy in a rabbit-hole. If we had two or three flights a day we considered ourselves lucky, very different from what we afterwards got in Holland.

Lubbock also records an amusing incident on his first ever visit to Didlington. Just as he joined the party, a cry was raised by several: 'Bring Mrs Waddington.' Two ladies in an open carriage leaned out anxiously watching, as again a cry arose: 'Here comes Mrs Waddington – now we shall see some sport.' Certainly this Mrs Waddington must have been something special to create such interest in the men present! She was indeed a favourite falcon.

There is no doubt that maintaining an establishment on such a large scale was an expensive undertaking, but the only record we have of subscriptions paid by members is in a letter from James Bots (falconer) to Edward Clough Newcome, dated London, 11 July 1835.

When I left Lord Berners and he settled with me, he was rather put out at having so much money to pay himself, and said he would let me know by letter, whether he would have the hawking next year. I find I can depend upon the £10 from the two gentlemen in London, for which I will be answerable, and as Col. Peel will give £30, that will [make] £50 with yours. Perhaps you will have the goodness to acquaint his Lordship with this, and then you would perhaps let me [know] as soon as possible how it is to be. You might also see Col. Peel on the subject, and I should take it as a great favour, in addition to what I have already received from you, if you will do me this kindness. As I should have to prepare, by taking the hawks at the latter end of August, I should be glad to hear about it soon.

Although only twenty-two years of age, Edward Newcome had already become involved with the financing and management of the club and also went to great lengths to obtain falcons for the flight at heron. He had a particular interest in gyrfalcons and in 1831 issued a handbill:

To Owners and Captains of Whalers and Vessels sailing in the Northern Seas.
  It frequently happens that Ships touch at Iceland, where the JERFALCON or ICELAND HAWK can be procured, and sometimes it has been caught in the rigging.

Following a minute description of a gyr, it continues:

If any person will forward a Hawk answering to the above description, in good plumage, without being in any way injured,

To Clough Newcome, Esq.,	Or To George Wyrley Birch, Esq.,
Hockwold,	Wretham,
Nr. Brandon,	Nr. Thetford,
Norfolk,	Norfolk,

He shall be paid TEN POUNDS.
  N.B. No other sort of Hawk will be paid for.
May 25th, 1831.

Even as early as the late 1820s, agricultural changes around Didlington were making it difficult for a large party of horsemen to follow flights. The great heathlands were slowly being broken up and brought under the plough and farmers could not accept the damage the followers might do to well grown corn in the hawking season – from April through to June. At the same time the draining of the fen country, the natural feeding grounds for a large company of herons, was to affect the previously regular passage of herons going out from, or returning to, the Didlington Hall heronry and so all too often a blank day would be the result. With Lord Berners's death early in 1838 the club lost its most influential landowner and the use of Didlington as the headquarters of the Falconer's Club.

The Renfrewshire Subscription Hawks

A second club, the Renfrewshire Subscription Hawks, had also emerged towards the end of the eighteenth century. This club had been started by Malcolm Fleming of Barochan, near Paisley in Renfrewshire. Fleming, born in 1745, was of a family long associated with the old sport, for had not an earlier Malcolm Fleming been presented with a hawk hood by James IV of Scotland on the occasion of a Barochan tiercel beating one of the King's falcons? This hood, in *cuir bouillé* ornamented with silver thread and seed pearls, was preserved by the family, but unfortunately the precious stones that had adorned the hood were stolen in the year of 1600. Exactly when the club came into being is not on record, but it is known that John Anderson, a celebrated Scottish falconer, was in club service in 1811 when James Howe of Edinburgh painted the well-known oil of Fleming on horseback, with Anderson and his assistant, George Harvey, with their falcons and dogs. Anderson, born in 1745, originally went to Barochan as assistant to John Hainshaw, but this must have been after 1798, at which time he was still in the employ of Sir Alexander Donne at Ochiltree. The club hawks were flown at woodcock and partridges and continued to be kept at Barochan after Fleming's death in 1819, under the mastership of Sir John Maxwell of Pollock, an enthusiastic and long-time member of the club. Anderson continued as falconer with Peter Ballantine to assist him until about 1830, when apparently the club came to an end. Both falconers were then employed by the Earl of Morton at Dalmahoy for two years, at the end of which Anderson retired, dying the following year.

Up to this date, the ancient line of Scottish falconers had managed their falcons in their own way. Great exponents of the training of eyases taken from their own cliffs for game hawking, they knew little of the Dutch methods of managing wild-caught falcons for the flight at kite or heron. When Anderson retired, Peter Ballantine was next employed by Lord Carmarthen as assistant to Jan Peels, who had been for some years with the Confederate Hawks at High Ash. Peels

16

Malcolm Fleming (mounted) and Anderson, his falconer.

kept a few passage falcons at work, Ballantine trained the Scottish eyases, and glorious sport was obtained at herons with the former and at every description of game with the latter. The noblest sport of all was the flight at woodcock, plentiful in the young plantations which then clothed Deeside – a flight which combined the glorious stoop of the well-placed game hawk with the high mounting or ringing flight usually obtained with the heron.

Thus it was that Ballantine had the opportunity to study the Dutch falconers' methods, as also did the Barrs, a notable family of Scottish falconers, when they too had the chance to work alongside the Dutchmen.

The Loo Hawking Club

With the death of Lord Berners and the loss of Didlington in 1838, it seemed that the Falconer's Club would have to close down. In the summer of that year, two members of the club, Mr Stuart-Wortley and the Baron d'Offemont, travelled to Holland at the suggestion of the Dutch falconer, Jan Bots, to look at the possibility of transferring their sport to the heathland and fens of that country. Encouraged by the enthusiastic report from those two gentlemen, the Duke of Leeds and Mr Newcome joined forces with them in 1839, with Jan Bots as head falconer, assisted by his brother 'Noll' Bots and Jan van der Boom. Twenty-one falcons were trained with which a total of one hundred and forty herons were taken. The ground over which they had obtained permission to fly was at the Loo near Apeldoorn and the following year, joined by other enthusiasts, a new club was founded, to be known as the Loo Hawking Club.

In the autumn of 1839, encouraged by the promise of the very best of heron hawking in such perfect country, Edward Newcome set out for Norway to trap passage gyrfalcons and in three weeks at Dovrefeld captured two male and one female gyr. Newcome was made secretary of the new club with Baron Tindall as president and the Prince of Orange and his brother, Prince Alexander, as patrons. Others among the thirty or so members were Prince Henry of the Netherlands, the Duke of Leeds, and Revd William Newcome, Lord Hamilton, Lord Strathmore, Mr Knight, Mr E. Green, Mr Stirling Crawford, Lord Suffield and the Hon. C. Fitzwilliam. Additional falconers were employed – 'Old Frank' van der Heuvell in 1840, James Bots, brother to 'Noll' and Jan, and Adrian Mollen in 1841. The rules for the new club were short but clearly to the point:

The Club shall be composed of members who will pay one hundred florins or more each year for the support of the Club.

Flying will take place in the Royal lands at the Loo, His Majesty having agreed to give his permission.

The season shall begin each year on the 10th May and continue until about 10th July.

The President shall choose a secretary and a treasurer to administer the affairs of the Club.

At the end of each season, on a day designated by the President, the treasurer shall give an account of the expenses for that year before the members meeting at the Hague.

The President is responsible for organizing the flying; in his absence the member of the longest standing will be Field Master.

The horses belonging to the Club are for the use of the Club falconers.

Flying will only take place on working days.

Members who wish to resign from the Club are obliged to notify the Secretary before the 1st September.

In order to become a member of the said Club it is necessary to be proposed by a member.

Karl Mollen.   *Paul Mollen.*

Zoe, *a gyrfalcon at the Royal Loo Club.*

19

In 1840 twenty-two falcons were trained and took one hundred and thirty-eight herons. The following year two groups of falconers were organised under Jan Bots and Adrian Mollen, and that season a total of two hundred and thirty-seven herons were taken with forty-four falcons. Again in that year, Jan Bots and van der Boom were sent by the club to the Dovre and trapped nine passage gyrfalcons in the course of four weeks. The following season one of these gyrs turned out well. Named *Zoe*, one of a team of forty-four falcons, she took eighteen of the hundred and forty-eight herons. Other famous falcons were trained over the following years, possibly the two best known being *Sultan* and *De Ruyter*, passage falcons of 1842. These falcons, trained by John Pells (English-born son of Jan Pells or Peels), then in the employ of Edward Newcome, took fifty-four herons in the summer of 1843. The following year this fine cast took a further fifty-seven herons. A new falcon named *Rocket*, which Newcome did not much care for, nevertheless took twenty-one herons single-handed. *De Ruyter* was unfortunately lost in 1844 on Lakenheath Warren, together with a second hawk. Flown as a cast at a rook, they were taken away downwind and went clean out of sight. *Sultan* remained as good as ever and in 1845 took three herons and twenty-five rooks. In that same year *Rocket* took two herons, twenty-five rooks, a wild duck and a seagull. *Cromwell* was another fine peregrine, but was lost flying a light heron singlehanded.

In the summer of 1845, the Duke of Leeds commissioned John Pells to go to Iceland to capture some gyrfalcons. After being detained for a fortnight in Copenhagen, he sailed for Iceland and reached Oniford on 7 July. He purchased half a dozen ponies to carry his baggage, nets and pigeons and eventually set out on a two-day ride to Bredemyre. Here he saw four Iceland falcons, and decided to build a trapping hut near by, setting up his poles and nets as used in Valkenswaard. Wishing to have two strings to his bow, he built a second trapping station about four miles from the first. The Iceland falcons were very tame, especially the birds of the year, who hardly seemed to regard man as an enemy. On one occasion, seeing some gyrs, Pells let go a pigeon on a twenty-five yard line and held the end. One of the young gyrs immediately took it.

On another occasion, a local boy came running to say that he had seen a gyr close by. Pells immediately supposed that one of the falcons he had already caught had escaped. However, it was a wild one and she was quickly taken in the bow-net, the falconer standing only fifteen yards away. This was towards the end of September. A few pigeons were kept at liberty about the huts and soon warned of the

Return from Hawking *by Landseer. The hawks on the cadge were drawn in Norfolk, using John Pell's hawks as models.*

approach of a falcon by dashing in to the hut the moment one came on the scene. One pair of gyrs which were about all the time that Pells was there would not come to the pigeon, no doubt having seen others trapped, but on one occasion when Pells flushed a pack of ptarmigan the gyrs each pursued and caught one. Pells shot plenty of plover, ducks and ptarmigan for the hawks; indeed, he must have worked extremely hard as he had no helper. By the end of September Pells had taken fifteen gyrs, but he had a difficult journey back to Oniford for it snowed heavily with much drifting. On 9 October he left Iceland and after a rough passage reached Copenhagen on the 26th, finally reaching Brandon in Suffolk on 19 November after an absence of nearly six months.

A few days later the Duke of Leeds came to see the gyrs and congratulated Pells on his great success and declared himself pleased that 'the sharks had not got him'. Eight of these lovely gyrs were given by the Duke of Leeds to the Loo Hawking Club, to be flown at heron. The remainder stayed in England with the duke, and Pells managed them for him.

Only one of the gyrs taken to the Loo turned out a good heron hawk and that was one of the jerkins (males) named *Morock*. In the spring of 1846, flown in a cast, he took twenty-four herons. The following season this jerkin was lost in Holland. He had been shot at

21

The Loo Hawking Club from a painting by Sonderland.

and wounded and was eventually recovered by Pells, who had been sent over to Holland for that purpose. Pells returned in triumph to Norfolk, where he moulted *Morock*, and killed several more herons with him, though he never flew as well as before the accident. One of the jerkins trained in England flew rooks and partridges well, but the females flown at hares were a failure.

In 1850 the club mews and headquarters were removed to the hunting lodge adjoining the royal palace at the Loo, and the king maintained, at his expense, one group of falconers under Adrian Mollen, the club continuing to be responsible for Jan Bots and his assistants, their falcons and the club horses.

The following year, one hundred and forty herons were taken with only eighteen falcons, but in 1852 the falconers had thirty-six falcons in their care with which they took a record two hundred and ninety-seven herons. About 1853 the Loo Club came to an end, the royal patronage was withdrawn and the headquarters closed down. One factor, noted by Newcome, which led to difficulties at the Loo was that the king insisted on dining at the very hour in the afternoon which was most favourable for hawking. Of necessity the whole court and members of the Loo Club had to follow the royal example.

The best eyewitness account of two days with the Loo Club was written by the Revd William Cyril Newcome, and printed in Freeman and Salvin's *Falconry*, published in 1859:

Loo, twelve o'clock, p.m. Scene, a bed-room at Marc Camphoo's Hotel. Falconer enters: – 'Not up, sir? Twelve o'clock. Wind S.W.; rain in the night, and cloudy now. Just a little wind. We must go to the Wesen field.'

A voice from the bed. – 'Open the window! What a fine day for hawking! Have all the hawks out! Tell them to get breakfast ready directly; some fish "bots", which they know how to cook so well.'

This speaker, and the rest of the members of the Club, had dined at the Palace yesterday, and managed somehow or other to get home late. However, they slept late, and arousing themselves at the falconer's call, got to the field by half past five. The falconers had been there with the hawks an hour or more, but no heron had passed – it was too hot. However, about six o'clock one was à la voléed, coming over very high. The falconers looked glum and undecided. *Sultan* and *De Ruyter* were ready on hand. The fortunate owner of these hawks cries out, 'Will you have a shy, James, or shall I?' The falconer addressed thinks it rather too high for his young hawks. 'Well, then, here goes,' says the former; and, having let the heron get a little past, off go the hoods. For a moment one hawk looks up, and is cast off; the other a moment or two afterwards. They both see him; now for a flight! The heron was about 250 yards high, and perhaps a quarter of a mile wide. The hawks had gone up about a quarter of the way before the heron saw them in hot pursuit. 'Now he sees them!' is exclaimed; and the riders rattle their horses as hard as they can, over deep sandhills, down wind. The heron, in the meanwhile, vomits up his fish to lighten himself, and begins ringing up down the wind. It is a curious thing to see the different manoeuvres of the birds. With his large wings, the heron can mount very fair, and has a far better chance of beating off the hawks than if he flew straight forward. This he knows full well by instinct, and puts on accordingly all sail for the upper regions, generally in short rings. Hawks make larger rings as a general rule, if, like these, they are good ones. Those have but a bad chance with a good heron, if they adopt the same tactics that he does in mounting. This the two old hawks know full well. So far they have been pretty near together, but seeing the prey beginning to mount, they separate, each their own way, now taking a long turn down wind, and then breasting the wind again. *De Ruyter* makes the best rings, and after having gone a mile, there is a shout – 'Now *De Ruyter* is above him!' and the hawk is seen poising herself for a stoop; down she comes, with closed wings, like a bullet and hits the heron; it is too high to see where, but the scream the quarry gives is tremendous. Hurrah! there's a stoop for you! Both hawk and heron have descended some yards; the former from the impetus of her stoop, much beneath the heron, but she shoots up again to a level. In fact, it was a perfect stoop. Though so near the heron she does not attempt a little stoop, but again heads the wind, so that the heron appears to be flying the hawk. *Sultan* is now above both, and makes her stoop, but not so good as her partner's. However, she makes two quickly, and is within an ace of catching; but the good heron will not

23

Prins von Orange, *a peregrine at the*
Royal Loo Club, from a painting
by Sonderland (1843).

Sultan, *another peregrine at*
the Royal Loo Club.

give an inch, and *Sultan* will have to make another ring for another stoop.
But where is *De Ruyter* all this time? She has made a long ring, and is now a
long way above them. She makes another full stoop, and this time there is no
mistake about it, for she hits the heron so hard that he is nearly stupefied.
Sultan joins in the fray and catches. 'Whoo-whoo-o-p!' down they come.
Down they all three go together, till, just before reaching the ground, the
two old hawks let go of their prey, which falls bump. Before he has had time
to recover himself, in a moment the hawks are on him, *De Ruyter* on the
neck, and *Sultan* on his body. Hurrah for the gallant hawks! and loud
whoops proclaim his capture. 'Wouldn't take 100*l*. for them' says their
owner, who has ridden well, judiciously as well as hard, and has got up in
time to save the heron's life. He gives the hawks a pigeon, and puts the heron
between his knees in a position so that he can neither spike him nor the
hawks with his bill. He has two beautiful long black feathers, which are duly
presented to Prince Alexander – alas! now no more – who is well up to the
take. These feathers are the badge of honour in heron-hawking in Holland
as the fox's brush is in hunting in England. The hawks are fed up as speedily

as possible, the heron has a ring put round his leg and is set loose, evidently not knowing what to make of it.

We hasten back as fast as we can, but the weather being now hot, the herons move more by night than by day. Many anxious eyes search the horizon for another. Opera-glasses are brought into requisition, and one gentleman called à la volée! to a gnat which got before the focus of his glass. At last two herons are viewed coming flapping lazily along. Every one is again on the alert, and the horses are mounted. It is a fair 'hood off' for the young hawks. A pretty little flight; and the result – the hawks fortunately sticking to the same bird – a capture. He is taken after having made about six or seven rings, and in ten stoops the whoop resounds. Peter, the other head falconer, has on hand two good hawks to fly, and all are wishing for a good heron to try their merits. In about half an hour one is seen coming rather wide; he has evidently been flown before, and now turns back down wind as hard as if the hawks were after him, being soon lost to sight. Great disappointment. In ten minutes another is à la voléed, and brought down in first-rate style. It is eight o'clock, and the falconers feed up. But the owner of *Sultan* and *De Ruyter* has a hawk called *Rocket*, which he does not care much about, as she is sure to crab another if flown with her; besides, she does not trouble herself after two or three stoops. This waiting 'just five minutes longer' ends with the take of another heron at the second stoop. We then scamper off as fast as we can to supper, the late hour of which accounts for our midday slumbers.

The next day was just the one we could have wished for the sport; for, as we had foretold, rain came the evening before, and there was plenty of herons flying. The wind was then S.W. and the field Wesen. About three o'clock we are there, and all the hawks, good, bad, and indifferent, are taken out – some to train who are backward, either from wildness or not taking kindly to heron; some who had been beaten off after long flights, or had been lost, and wanted entering again. About twenty-eight are on the cadges: they begin with a 'train' – i.e. a bagged heron – on the way; but, like a bagged fox, it is not good for much, and is soon taken. A little better flight with the next 'train', and the hawks are promised to fly a wild one tomorrow. These two herons then receive their liberty, but would not fly at first a hundred yards at a time, evidently expecting to be pounced on again.

Here we are at the field; hitherto we have been only on the way to it. The two sets of falconers, with their hawks, place themselves about half a mile apart, to intercept the herons on their passage back from their fishing grounds. 'À la volée' is called; it is for Peter; a pretty little flight is the result. The amateurs' horses have hardly time to catch their wind before James is seen just hooding off at another, and we have another flight of much the same sort with a catch. We have just time to light our pipes and get through the best part of one before we are disturbed by another 'À la volée'. A heron is coming very low; immediately he sees the hawks on wing he vomits up a good-sized eel, and is trying to do the same with something else. Of course he falls an easy victim, for he has a pike of nearly two pounds in his throat, and the head of which being downwards, has been digested. The eel is found entire, and is reserved by one of the falconers for supper. Another comes Peter's way, and is bagged; another to James, which escapes – for, as soon as the two hawks are well on the wing, one 'crabs' the other, and they fall fighting to the ground. The heron goes on his way to his expectant family, not even having thought it worthwhile to throw up the fish. Peter has another chance, but after a few stoops the hawks give up. The truth is they are reserving the best birds for the arrival of the Royal party. However, six flights, with four catches in one hour and thirty-six minutes, afforded some nice sport.

The Royal party is now seen approaching, some in carriages and some on horseback – a very pretty turn-out. Two casts are on hand, and, as luck will have it, a heron immediately flies close by. After a short flight of half a dozen rings and stoops, the hawks and heron tumble down within a few hundred yards of the Royal carriages. One amateur rushes to secure the heron, who gives him a hint of 'noli me tangere' by striking him with his bill close to the eye – a spot herons always aim at. They must be secured by the neck. Another young gentleman, anxious to show the bird's graceful plumage to the royal party, takes hold of the heron, but not scientifically, for, after walking a few yards, he feels the heron's bill in the back part of his neck, and blood is drawn. He gets laughed at, but holds the bird pluckily. Somebody comes to the rescue and holds the bill, while the black feathers are plucked out and presented to the Queen; also divers plumes to the dames d'honneur. The bird is then dismissed, with much pity from the ladies.

There is no lack of herons. The little wind there was has fallen to a calm, and they come home higher. All the better, for we have some good casts to fly. One is 'hooded off' at, and, after a capital flight, is taken high in the air. The pet hawks are now taken in hand – *De Ruyter* and *Sultan*; and, as there is no wind, the owner says he will fly at the first 'light one' that comes at all fair. All is excitement when one is seen coming from the heronry, and therefore unweighted. They are 'hooded off' in his face; he sees them directly, and proceeds to mount. 'Now, good hawks, you will have some work to do before you overtake him!' The knowing riders are down wind as hard as they can go. Ring after ring is made, and yet the hawks seem to gain but little on him. Still they are flying like swallows: *De Ruyter* makes a tremendous ring, but still fails to get above him. Again and again they ring, and have attained a great height. A scream of delight is heard: 'They are above him; *De Ruyter* is at him!' A fine stoop, but the heron dodges out of the way. Now for *Sultan*; but she misses too: the heron is up like a shot, and three or four rings have to be made before there is another stoop. Another and another stoop, with loud cheers from below. *Sultan* just catches him once, but can't hold: it seems still a doubtful victory, when *De Ruyter* hits him hard; and, after two or three more stoops, *Sultan* catches him, amidst the excitement of hurrahs and whoops. A really good flight: can't be better – two and a half miles from

*The Queen of Holland rides side-saddle on the galloping horse
at the left; the King is in the centre of the picture, looking on
while Jan Bots makes in to capture the heron.*

where they are 'hooded off'.

We return well satisfied with the sport, and scarcely in time to see another flight going on; still they come over our heads, making a great quantity of stoops, but the young hawks are too eager, and hang at him too much; but they are good plucked ones, and at length pull him down: unfortunately the heron falls with such force that he kills himself. Another comes at a good height, and seeing the hawks as soon as they are off the hand, sets off mounting immediately, after getting rid of his fish. It will be a fine flight if the hawks stick to him, but he is very high before they reach him; they make three or four stoops and then fall below him some distance. They are so high, they look the size of swallows. One makes another stoop and then gives up; the other sticks to him, and is at last entirely lost to sight – soon afterwards we cannot see the heron; but shrill screams are heard, and the hawk has not given him up yet. The other hawk is taken down to a pigeon. We stand still gazing up, but see nothing more, and the plucky but deserted hawk is taken up half an hour after. A cast or two more are flown, and 'homeward' is the word to dinner, at half-past nine.

Thus ended as good a day's sport as any one could wish to see. Bumpers of champagne were quaffed to the health of the Royal Family, and the Royal Loo Club; nor were the healths of *Sultan* and *De Ruyter* forgotten.

Alas! we shall never see such sport again; for the club is broken up, and probably the heronry destroyed.

2
SALISBURY PLAIN

With the finish of the Loo Hawking Club, the continuation of falconry rested heavily on the shoulders of Edward Clough Newcome, who was undoubtedly the most able and skilful of amateur falconers. In 1852, Newcome moved house from Hockwold to Feltwell Hall and was often to be seen in that part of the country with a hawk on hand, accompanied by a boy to carry the cadge and perhaps unhood a second hawk. John Pells, living at nearby Hockwold, was usually out as well, but he seldom handled Newcome's hawks, nor Mr Newcome his.

When hawking, Edward Newcome used to ride a very clever pony he had brought from Holland, a dark chestnut mare with a great deal of white about her face, making her most conspicuous. It was commonly remarked that the local rooks could recognise the pony and would keep their distance, making it difficult to get close enough to slip a rook-hawk at them – a remark that apparently had some truth in it. When hawking on the warrens, where the ground from its sandy soil was honeycombed with rabbit holes, making it most dangerous for horsemen, this pony showed great intelligence in avoiding the worst places and if she did slip into a hole always managed to stay upright and stood still until extricated.

Newcome still managed a few flights at heron; indeed, in 1854 he successfully entered two eyas falcons to this difficult quarry. These two falcons, *Verbaea* and *Vengeance*, had been well hacked and entered to grouse. Newcome said of *Verbaea* that she was the swiftest eyas and nearly, if not quite, the fastest peregrine he had ever seen. She was always first up to the heron, even when flown with one of his best passage falcons, despite the fact that she flew without the first primary in each wing, lost in an accident. She was a very large falcon, but her great pace was the best of her, she not being particularly bold and a clumsy footer. These falcons had been hacked in Yorkshire by Captain Francis Henry Salvin, another falconer who did much to ensure the survival of the old sport. Rooks afforded the next best flight, and from the beginning of March until the corn was well grown Newcome could be met with in the open country around Hockwold, Wilton and Feltwell. He even succeeded, after many failures, in establishing a rookery near to Feltwell Hall. Later in the season he would resort to Lakenheath and Wangford warrens in Suffolk, and here, besides rooks, he had the occasional flight at stone curlew. Sometimes the hawks were taken into the fens for a chance at a carrion crow or magpie. When the cornfields were cleared he would fly a merlin or two at larks, a sport he ranked only second to heron hawking, the ringing flight at a lark and heron being similar. But he had little time for game hawking or the short-winged hawks. On one occasion William Barr, elder brother to John and Robert, all well-known Scottish falconers, visited Edward Newcome at Hockwold. William Barr at that time was travelling through England exhibiting his hawks at racecourses and other public places. So thoroughly tame were his hawks that on one occasion Mr Newcome and a young friend, Alfred Newton, went out snipe shooting with Barr, who had a falcon flying nearly all the time to make the snipe lie, which they did, it being almost impossible to make them rise. They killed a great many but thought it not much sport.

Although Newcome was undoubtedly the backbone of falconry after the closing down of the Loo Hawking Club, there were others who played their small part in ensuring its survival. Mention has already been made of John Pells, who, on retiring on a pension from the Duke of St Albans, Hereditary Grand Falconer of England, hacked and trained a few eyas peregrines each year, some for young gentlemen falconers. Norfolk has never been a stronghold for nesting peregrines, there being few suitable cliffs in the county, although as late as 1815 the Hunstanton Cliffs had held an eyrie, well known to the local falconers. However, Pells's father, when in the employ of John Dawson Downes of Old Gunton Hall near Yarmouth, took eyases from the steeple of Corton Church near Lowestoft, in the 1820s. They continued to breed there for a few years, Dawson Downes paying the church clerk a small retainer to preserve them.

In 1843, John Pells made a sporting tour with the young Francis Henry Salvin, through the North of England, with hawks and dogs, following the example of Colonel Thornton in 1786. Captain Salvin (born 4 April 1817 at Croxdale Hall, Durham), on leaving Ampleforth College, had made the acquaintance of old John Tong, who for

Francis Henry Salvin.   *John Barr.*

some years had been an assistant falconer to Colonel Thornton, and from Tong Salvin acquired his love of falconry. On their tour they enjoyed excellent sport with Mr Riddell of Leyburn, Mr Marmaduke Salvin, of Burn Hall on Edmondbyer Moors, and Mr Silvertop at Minsteracres. On another occasion, again taking Pells, they went to Linton, where they had partridge hawking with some good tiercels and a noted setter named Rake.

In 1853, Captain Salvin engaged young John Barr, then a lad of twelve, as falconer. John Barr, born in 1840, acquired his taste for hawking from his father, William, as did his brothers, William and Robert. William, the eldest brother, a powerful man of six feet three inches, came out as a falconer in 1850 and, as already mentioned, spent much of his time exhibiting hawks about the country. He was an excellent shot and could kill a grouse with the gun held in one hand while he carried a falcon on the other. In the summer of 1853 he was employed by Sir Charles Slingsby, who had taken Fewston Moor in Yorkshire for the grouse hawking, Captain Salvin being nearby at Kilnsey, near Skipton.

The two brothers had with them a good lot of eyases, hacked at Minard Castle, and these were flown with some success, one named *Snapdragon* turning out especially well. In the autumn of that year William emigrated to Australia, but John remained in the service of Salvin, hawking a good deal in Lancashire at Claughton Hall. On

30

Maharajah Dhuleep Singh.   *Robert Barr.*

Captain Salvin's regiment being posted to Ireland in 1855, he and John Barr perfected the art of magpie hawking, taking seventy-four magpies in enclosed country near to the Cahir Barracks in Tipperary.

In the autumn of 1857 Salvin and Barr again visited Ireland, this time enjoying excellent sport in the countryside around Clonmel in Tipperary and in Cork and Kildare. The meets were advertised in the local papers to encourage a field, so necessary as an aid in magpie hawking. With two tiercels, *Dhuleep Singh* and *The O'Donohue*, they took 184 magpies in about four months. Both these tiercels were excellent at their job, though very different in style. *The O'Donohue* always killed from a hard stoop, cutting his magpie over. *Dhuleep Singh* would come in behind his quarry and bind to it, although he could stoop well enough. They were also most successful at rooks over the same country, with three falcons *Hydra*, *Assegai*, and *Azrael*, who took a total of sixty-eight rooks and a crow. On the last day of sport in Tipperary, *Dhuleep Singh* took eight magpies singlehanded.

On leaving Captain Salvin in 1857, John Barr was engaged by the

Maharajah Dhuleep Singh and remained in his employ for eight years. During that time he travelled with the Maharajah through Italy, Egypt and India, in the last country showing great sport at wildfowl and game with a variety of hawks. Much of the time he was in the company of Lt-Col. Delmé Radcliffe, and returned home with him overland in April 1862 in charge of twelve fine falcons.

The youngest of the three Barr brothers was Robert, who for a time worked as assistant to John, both with Captain Salvin and the maharajah. In 1863, the Hon. Cecil Duncombe, with Robert as falconer, together with Major Charles Hawkins Fisher, began rook hawking on Salisbury Plain using the Bustard Inn as their head-quarters. The following year they again organised rook hawking in the same country on a more ambitious scale, importing ten passage falcons from Mollen at Valkenswaard. Not only did they enjoy the best of sport at rooks, but they also witnessed a remarkable flight at a peewit by a wild peregrine, well described by Major Fisher:

Well do I remember the day, March 30th, 1864, as I see by my diary. The morning was wintry enough, a constant and wearisome succession of snow-storms, and I was sitting alone in the then well-known Bustard Inn, which still stands by the side of the old road from Salisbury to Devizes and just half-way between these towns. The country around was perfectly open, and with hardly a fence in the twenty miles. I was then engaged there in rook hawking, and the hawks were under the care of the well-known young Scotch falconer, Robert Barr, and consisted of a capital lot of six or seven passage falcons (all red hawks), and the first that had been imported for many years for hawking purposes from Mollen, the Dutch hawk-catcher. Little cared Barr for reading or writing, or for any indoor occupation in the daytime. The storms of snow long prevented him from taking out, either for use or for exercise, any of these hawks, but in the afternoon, in a sort of lull – the sky being full of the lurid mauve-coloured clouds that often accompany a downland snowy day – Barr fidgeted so much that he persuaded me to accompany him, with but one hawk on his fist, in quest of a chance at a rook. It was a very unwise proceeding, for very soon after we had left the inn for the Netheravon Downs a short but furious snowstorm obliged us to seek shelter in a thick plantation of Scotch fir. The storm passed away, and just as we were thinking of moving out, there floated by us, quite close, a fine old peregrine falcon, her breast bleached by age perchance, but I think mainly by weather, almost to the colour of the snow itself. In a moment she was gone, and we again prepared to move. 'How I should like, Robert,' quoth I, 'to have one more look at that fine old falcon as near as that.' 'You have your wish, sir,' said he, 'for here she comes again', pointing to something seen with his keen eyes in the far distance. Out came my field-glasses, and there, sure enough, coming rapidly downwind and straight towards us, was a wild peregrine, though certainly not the bird we had just seen, hotly engaged with a wild peewit, and every instant coming nearer and nearer. Luckily we had not yet deserted our shelter in the plantation, and soon discovered that the advancing hawk was an old wild tiercel, most probably the mate of the falcon just seen. Barr and I were delighted at this chance; for though we had seen the skeleton of many a peewit which a wild hawk had killed and partly eaten, and on this very down had frequently watched some wild peregrine try hard, but in vain, to catch a peewit by repeated stoops, we had never seen a 'kill', and had constantly wondered and talked of how the thing was done. On every occasion of this kind we had seen the peregrine follow her usual mode of attack, and execute brilliant stoops, which, however, were always successfully evaded by the peewit, and the flight given up by the falcon, so far as we could observe. As for mounting, few birds do it easier or better, and none, methinks, so well evade the falcon's stoop as our friend the peewit. This particular flight, however, was worked in a totally different fashion, and entirely down the wind, which was not high.

I know not how the hawk may have begun this flight before the birds came into sight; but, so far as we could see it, not one single stoop did he attempt. In lieu of stooping, a most effective and to us unusual manoeuvre was adopted. When coming to close quarters, instead of stooping from above, the tiercel always rushed up from below, turned over, and tried to grab the peewit. He was, of course, easily enough 'put out', as we expected, by the turns and twists of the hunted bird. No whit discouraged, time after time the hawk went upward in the air for a few yards only after his miss, and then hurled himself downward after, and far faster than his quarry, passed over him and then headed him by some twenty yards or so. The peewit, with the hawk thus waiting for him down-wind, and close at hand, did not dare to hang in the wind, or to fly against if for a single second of time. He had, therefore, no alternative but to go on down-wind as best he could. There lay his adversary, ready and waiting for him; but the only resource possible to the hunted bird was to elude by some means the hawk's next upward rush and attempted clutch. It came, and grandly was it delivered. Just opposite to us the birds seemed to touch; and there, we knew, were the ready feet and sharp pounces to be reckoned with, but, nevertheless, to be as grandly evaded by the peewit. Again and yet again, rose the hawk from beneath, always intent upon grabbing, and again and again did the peewit turn over, like a great grey moth (or an oyster-shell, according to Robert Barr), just, and only just, to avoid the deadly clutch for a few minutes longer. But his last hour was at length come. It was quite evident to us that this was too hot to last, as upon every repulse, instead of giving the flight up with discomfiture, the hawk hurled himself with yet greater vigour and fury right over his quarry, and waylaid him some few yards down-wind as before; whilst the ground was entirely free from covert, and it was clear that the peewit would do himself no good, but harm, by essaying to mount. As we were comparatively near the two birds, which were evidently too much engaged with

33

their struggle to heed us, we were able to see fully six or eight of these beautiful attempts by the hawk, which clearly were deliberately planned by him, and included none of the stoops which we had till then supposed to be the peregrine's method of catching the peewits we had seen lying dead. Finally (as was to be expected), the peewit seemed to get tired and frightened, and tried to come back up-wind towards the fir covert, which luckily concealed us. This sealed his fate. Up came the tiercel grabbing again, and this time with full success. The two birds met and did not part, for down came the hawk on to the open green down, holding the peewit in his foot. I could stand the sight no longer; but, mounting my horse, galloped out from the trees. I came so quickly to the hawk that he was forced to let his quarry go unhurt. Away rose the peewit, and soon afterwards the hawk. As it was then, of course, 'all out' with the poor peewit, he had not put many score yards between himself and his enemy (who evidently did not want or mean to lose him) before the latter went for him again, rose quite leisurely over him, this time to a sufficient height in the air, and then, by as lovely a stoop as ever I saw delivered, cut him down stone-dead on the turf before my eyes. I now regret to add that we did not after all allow the hawk to keep his well-earned quarry, for Barr came up and frightened him off it, took it up, and put it in his pocket, remarking that he could easily get another for himself.

The Major, much impressed by the flight at the peewit, wrote a report to his good friend A. E. Knox, the author of *Game Birds and Wildfowl* and other books, who had earlier returned to London:

10, Eaton Place West,
London S.W.
April 3rd.

Dear Captain Fisher,
Many thanks for your letter from the Bustard Inn, which has interested me very much – I quite envy your having witnessed that wonderful flight with the wild tiercel and the peewit. I cannot help thinking that a passage tiercel might be successfully trained to the sport, and the peewits are so numerous on the Salisbury Plain that there would be no lack of quarry – three tiercels entered to peewits would vary a day's sport immensely – However I suppose there would be considerable danger of losing a passage bird. I suppose you will have the peewit mounted – you ought to do so, to perpetuate the memory of such a sporting incident – I thought that you would find a difficulty about showing Mr. Raikes any sport on account of the boisterous weather. Even in London the sound of the wind in the chimneys for many nights last week quite overpowered the roll of the cabs in the street. How fortunate it was that you recovered the eyasses – Duncombe will be pleased

to hear the account of *Druid*'s exploit and recovery which I suppose you will have sent him.

Many thanks for your good wishes. The morning of the 31st broke auspiciously for the wedding, and everything went off more smoothly and successfully than I had ventured to anticipate. I was on horseback yesterday for the first time, on 'Silvertail', since his and my return to London. I took one turn in Rotten Row and then back to the stables in digust. It was a sad contrast to galloping after the glorious *Hurricane* and *Favourite*, or watching *Juno* in the clouds. I address this to Stroud as you mentioned that you were to leave the Bustard the day after you wrote. Believe me

Yours very truly,
A. E. Knox.

Hurricane was a remarkable young passage falcon, sent over from Holland with nine others, after the autumn migration of 1863. Robert Barr brought them over and trained them for the start of the rook-hawking season in March 1864. *Hurricane* was entered to rooks on 16 March in what proved to be a wild and stormy year. This

Major Fisher and C.E. Radclyffe with two of their grouse hawks on the moor.

falcon, which displayed extraordinary speed and high mounting, together with a great certainty of stoop, continued to kill rooks with great enthusiasm for weeks, then suddenly refused to notice them at all. She was a very calm and easily managed falcon, large, and of a beautiful appearance. Unlike most young falcons, she had retained the slate-coloured bloom of the fresh-taken eyas, and differed little from the colour of the adult falcon on back and wings; the ground colour of her breast and underparts was also unusually pale, with a large almost white patch in the centre of the breast.

Tiercels, as a rule, are normally considered too small to manage a rook. *Druid*, an eyas tiercel of 1863, belonging to Cecil Duncombe, visited Ireland in the autumn of that year and was entered to magpies. In the spring, he entered well to rooks, and for three years took his turn with first-class teams of passage falcons.

The Birth of the Old Hawking Club

From these small beginnings, a club was organised which was called the Old Hawking Club. The Hon. Cecil Duncombe, who was a captain in the 1st Life Guards from 1861 to 1867, finding he had little enough time to manage the club, encouraged Edward Clough Newcome to shoulder that responsibility, the membership at the end of 1864 being:

Capt. the Hon. C. Duncombe,
Lord Lilford,
The Maharajah Dhuleep Singh,
A. E. Knox,
Colonel Brooksbank,
Mr Amhurst,
Mr E. C. Newcome.

The spring rook hawking soon became the main feature of the diary for members of the Old Hawking Club, although a little heron hawking was still attempted in May, when the club falcons and falconer returned to Norfolk. Soon further enthusiasts were invited to join in the sport and a young man of seventeen years, the Hon. Gerald Lascelles, was present in the spring of 1866 and much enjoyed all that he saw.

The previous year, John Barr, who for eight seasons had travelled the world as Dhuleep Singh's falconer, secured an engagement with

Lord Lilford.   *Trapped at Valkenswaard.*

the Vicomte de Grandmaison, at the Château des Souches in France, and in February 1866 was employed as head falconer to a new club, organised by Monsieur Pierre Pichot, to be called 'The Champagne Hawking Club'. The headquarters were at Châlons, where the emperor Napoleon III had specially authorised the use of falcons, and great sport was shown on the fine plain nearby at rooks, magpies, stone curlews, little bustards and occasional herons. The mews housed seventeen peregrines, passagers and eyases, two female goshawks, two Barbary lanners and two hobbies.

In the autumn of 1867, Comte Alphonse de Aldama and Pierre Pichot journeyed to Valkenswaard, taking Barr with them, and spent some time with Adrian Mollen, trapping and training the passage hawks.

The Champagne Club also visited Normandy, where they were entertained by the Comte de Canteleu at the Château St-Martin, and enjoyed good sport at rooks, which were numerous, as were magpies. But the open plains of the Vexin, once the hawking grounds of the kings of France, were now much enclosed. In 1869, Comte Alphonse de Aldama took over the presidency from M. Alfred Werlé, keeping the hawks at Chantilly, until he went to live in Havana when the club was broken up. Barr was obliged to return to England, where,

Members of the Old Hawking Club.

shortly, he joined his brother Robert, then in the service of Lord Bute. They had some excellent passage hawks that John had brought with him from France and these, together with some eyas falcons, were taken to Grandtully Castle, at the invitation of the Maharajah Dhuleep Singh, for grouse hawking. John Barr reported: 'We are having the finest grouse hawking here that has ever been seen, killing three or four brace a day, but our hawks are too good – they kill every time they are flown, very often far out of sight, and are not found the same day, and often are difficult to take up after they have been left out one night.' One of the best hawks in the team was a very old haggard called *Granny*, who had been equally good at heron, but the star performer in the team was a very small passage falcon named *Aurora*.

In the summer of 1869, Maharajah Dhuleep Singh sent his falconer Jamie Barr (a nephew of John's), together with John, to Iceland to procure some gyrfalcons. The Barrs were most successful and returned with thirty-three of these most lovely falcons to Elvedon, the home of Dhuleep Singh, Maharajah of Lahore. The maharajah was the son of 'The Lion of the Punjab', Runjeet Singh, and succeeded him when only one year old. He lost his throne, made his home in Suffolk, with a generous pension from the government, was a great favourite with Queen Victoria, and turned the Elvedon estate into one of the finest partridge grounds in the country.

After the rook hawking in the spring of 1869, Robert Barr left the Old Hawking Club and was employed by the Marquis of Bute. After the successful grouse hawking at Grandtully, referred to above,

A falconer with cadge in France.

Lunch while rook hawking on the Plain. Lascelles is behind hamper.

Robert returned to Cardiff Castle with Lord Bute's hawks, but in September he was taken ill, and his brother John replaced him as falconer. The following spring, apparently much improved in health, Robert was again rook hawking on the plain, in company of Gerald Lascelles, where they had a certain amount of sport. Robert Barr died in 1871 and on 22 September that same year Edward Clough Newcome also died at Feltwell Hall. The great services rendered by him to the noble art of falconry would be hard to evaluate. An active member of the Falconry Club at Didlington, Secretary to the Anglo-Dutch Royal Loo Hawking Club and manager of the infant Old Hawking Club, he was always ready to help anybody interested in the sport and to give advice from his great experience to young and old, high or low. It was written of him:

The kind landlord, the hospitable neighbour, in short, the English squire of the old school, yet exists in plenty; but falconry in the British Isles will scarcely again find such a patron and pillar of strength as in the true-hearted gentleman who, before he attained middle age, was affectionately greeted by that single English epithet which at once expresses the veneration felt towards a superior, the honest admiration of an equal, and the thorough appreciation of good fellowship; for at lordly board or in lady's bower, double-barrel in hand, or hawk on fist, the cheerful countenance, the genial humour, and the animating presence of 'Old Clough' were ever welcome.

3
THE
MEETING

With the early death of 'Old Clough', the Old Hawking Club, already at a low ebb, suffered a severe blow. Little had been done in the two previous seasons in the way of rook hawking and the club had no falconer, hawks or headquarters.

However, in the late autumn of 1871, Cecil Duncombe, A. E. Knox and Gerald Lascelles held a meeting at Gordon Castle and there agreed to try to reorganise the Old Hawking Club on a more substantial basis. Gerald Lascelles, on accepting the position of Hon. Secretary and Manager, approached Colonel Brooksbank, Lord Lilford and others of the original membership for additional support, and he wrote to John Barr and secured him as falconer for the spring season on Salisbury Plain.

It was too late to obtain any passage hawks from Mollen in Holland, but Barr agreed to supply suitable hawks and a start was made in March 1872. Gerald Lascelles travelled down to the Bustard Inn, arriving in the morning of 25 March, to find Cecil Duncombe already 'at home' with John Barr, an assistant and a team of eight hawks. Of these, four were peregrine falcons, one a moulted hawk, who was already flying well and killing, but the most promising of the red falcons was bad with the 'croaks'. These were all eyas falcons. A very pretty little passage tiercel, caught three weeks earlier, was already fairly tame, but a second tiercel, a nestling, was not of much account. The two remaining hawks were Iceland falcons, neither much good, one especially having a damaged wing.

On the evening of the 26th, more hawks arrived from Ireland, on loan to Lascelles from Mr Corbet - two Iceland gyrs, a male and a female, and four peregrine tiercels, one a passager trapped in Ireland and the others all nestlings that had been flown at magpies in the autumn with some success. That same evening, a fine wild falcon flew over the inn and both Lascelles and Barr rushed to the hut in hopes of trapping her, but she did not stop.

The weather at the beginning of the season was unkind to them, with storms and strong winds, but improved towards the end, the season finishing on 15 April. On 3 April Captain Hawkins Fisher had joined the party, bringing with him a further two hawks – a good falcon, and a nice tiercel that had been imported from Africa.

The 'blue' falcon proved a difficult hawk, given to soaring and self-hunting, and much time was spent in searching for her, fortunately always successfully, although on one occasion the boy took her up on a rook seven miles downwind, beyond Stonehenge. *The Moor*, Captain Fisher's African tiercel, and *Limerick*, one of Corbet's eyas tiercels, flew well, both at rooks and magpies. *Miss Simmonds*, the best of the three red falcons, flew well in a cast with Fisher's falcon, and *The Redman* and *The Rake*, the other two Irish eyases, did some good work at magpies. On one occasion the 'blue' falcon killed two rooks in one flight. On being slipped, she raked off downwind and killed a rook at a great height in the air with one stoop, the rook falling stone dead into a crowd of people; the falcon went on downwind and killed again. In riding hard after her, Lascelles had a crashing fall, the winded pony cast on top of him for some time, but there was no serious damage to either man or beast. On 12 April a 'lawn meet' was held at Tilshead. As Lascelles noted, 'A deal of "quality" out – Sir Francis Astley and sons (with a carriage full of lunch) and various military officers'. The day went well, with two kills, *The Moor* going particularly well and killing high in the air. The 'blue' falcon soared away as usual and was lost, but fortunately was recovered the following day when she was seen loafing about over the rookery at Camdown. The expenses for the season were £100 paid to Barr, this to cover the cost of supplying the hawks, equipment and pony.

The season of 1872 had not been a great success. A total of only twenty-six head of quarry was taken by a moderate team of hawks, and Lascelles, determined to do better, ordered fresh passage falcons and tiercels from Mollen for the following season. A particularly fine team of hawks was got together, the passage tiercels including two remarkably good ones, *The Earl* and *The Doctor*, which took a few wild peewits, an exceedingly difficult bird. Of the passage falcons, three were of the highest class. *The Empress*, a long, light-red hawk with a light slaty bloom to her feathers, *Dutch Lady* and *The Duck-killer*. The last only came into the sweep of the trapper's net by chance, as Gerald Lascelles reported:

The Meeting

He [Adrian Mollen] had just caught a falcon, and was taking her out of the net when there came up, attracted by the pigeon, an exceedingly fine dark falcon. It was too late to hide, but when, an hour or so afterwards, she again appeared at the scene, and he pulled out the lure pigeon, all that resulted was, that after a shy stoop the falcon followed the line at the height of a yard or two right from the net to the hut, spread her wings and sailed away. There were many wild fowl on the heath at the time, and he could see this grand hawk day after day chasing and killing them in the finest style, till his mouth fairly watered to catch her. In vain did he try all his arts; every time he showed his lure the crafty bird would sail along the extended string, as if to show how well she understood the game, and then would bid him good-bye. Worst of all, she would brook no intruder on her hunting grounds, and day after day as other falcons passed and began to stoop to the pigeon, she would descend upon them from the clouds, and after a buffeting match would drive them away. Mollen was in despair, the season was slipping away, and his business being lost. At last he took his gun to the hut, having made up his mind to shoot the hawk as a last resource and free himself from the incubus. Hour after hour he sat with gun in readiness – a strange position, indeed, for a falconer. But that day she came not, nor the next, and at last the gun was laid aside and the hawk catching went on as before.

At the end of the week one of Mollen's sons who was working a hut many miles away returned home with his catch. He had not much to boast of, except one, 'a real beauty'. Hardly had the old man set eyes on her than he recognised his tormentor – unmistakable from her size, dark plumage, and beauty. She had gone straight to the other hut after plaguing him the last day he saw her, but never having been frightened at that place, was less suspicious and was so caught. This hawk came into the possession of the Old Hawking Club, where she was known as *The Duck-killer*, and was one of the grandest hawks for temper, flying qualities, and steadiness that the Club have ever owned, killing over forty rooks her first season. She was eventually lost when flying rooks at Feltwell in Norfolk and it is to be hoped became the mother of falcons as good as herself on some wild cliff in North Britain, or Scandinavia.

The Empress was the star of the very fine team of rook hawks. From the very first she showed a great fondness for rooks, but at the start was inclined to soar and seek for her own opportunity. However, this habit soon wore off and she became a persevering, honest and extremely effective rook hawk and probably the most useful the club had ever possessed. *The Empress* took forty-seven rooks, the score for the season being one hundred and thirty-two. In the autumn *The Empress* was taken with other hawks to Ireland, where she was flown in enclosed and much-wooded country with remarkable success, rarely failing to kill. It was perhaps here that this falcon learned her

John Frost, aged fourteen, at Stonehenge in 1868.

John Frost, the mature man.

extraordinary cunning and clever footing, which enabled her to kill sixty-five rooks in her second season of 1874.

The Old Hawking Club was now well established. The spring rook hawking was the major feature of the year, and in 1873 Lascelles and Salvin, together with the club falconers, had enjoyed a sporting tour in Ireland, with some rook hawking, excellent magpie hawking and further attempts at peewits on the Curragh. The position of head falconer was now taken by John Frost, Barr leaving in the winter of 1873 to be employed by Captain Dugmore, the nineteen-year-old son of Michael Frost, head keeper to the late Edward Newcome. Brought up among hawks at Feltwell, John and his elder brother, Alfred learnt much of hawking from John Pells and Robert Barr, young John travelling to Wiltshire as assistant to Robert when but twelve years of age.

The membership of the Club had increased to nine: the Earl of Craven, Lord Lilford, the Hon. G. R. C. Hill, the Hon. C. W. Fitzwilliam, the Hon. Cecil Duncombe, F. H. Salvin, A. Brooksbank Esq., F. Newcome, Esq., and the Hon. Gerald Lascelles. The club hawks being kept, when not hawking, at Lascelles home at Oakhurst on the family estate near to Leeds.

Frost's first season proved most successful, the rook hawks taking the grand total of one hundred and eight rooks. *Empress* took the pride of place with her record score, closely followed by *Pearl* and *Turquoise*, all three falcons being put by to moult for the following season. In the autumn a further tour was made in Ireland with a team of nine hawks and *Medusa*, the club goshawk, provided some sport during the summer.

The weather was to spoil sport in the spring of 1875. It was very bad at times and the wind made it difficult to get near enough to rooks to give the young hawks a chance at them. One of the most promising of the young falcons was unfortunately shot:

Friday, April 2nd. Did not fly hawks, as J. Frost went to look for *Bellona*, who was shot the day before by a bailiff – she was seen to kill three rooks there – *Diana* still at large, killed a rook between Beache's Barn and Everleigh. Saturday April 3rd. *Diana* caught a rook when close and a snare was set on it at 6.30 a.m. She was caught at 3.30 p.m.
Tuesday, April 6th. First advertised meet at Netheravon. Fair congregation. Very strong wind from W. with heavy showers. *Pearl* flew a fine flight in morning in the valley but failed to kill, owing to the wind and a large 'field' – would not fly in the afternoon. *Empress* refused twice. *Rowena* flew a fine flight near the rookery at Stagg's Gorse – killed high in the air her third stoop . . . Friday May 7th. Met at Easton to meet Lady Aylesbury and party who did not arrive. Very windy and stormy. *Pearl*, *Empress* and *Rowena* each killed in fine style – *Empress* flying a fine ringing flight. Only had three flights.

The hawks were only flown for about a month and accounted for fifty-nine head of quarry. Nevertheless, Lascelles and Frost were pleased with some of the falcons. *Pearl* flew in very fine form throughout the season; *Rowena*, a very fine tall hawk, when once in form never lost it, and if moulted well would prove invaluable the following season; *Diana* was unlucky in being lost so often, but flew in a style that few hawks could surpass; *Bellona* would have been the best of the lot if she had not been shot; *Empress* at times flew in a queer way, but when she chose to exert herself her flying was in the grandest style. Sadly, on the last day of the season, *Empress* was lost after a rook. Two days later nothing had been seen or heard of her, although members searched all the country around. Lascelles left Frost at Everleigh to continue to search for her. He had no success. In summing up her career, Lascelles wrote:

Empress – one of the best hawks, and perhaps the most useful the Old Hawking Club has ever possessed . . . It was in 1874 in Wilts that she was at

A passage falcon belonging to the Old Hawking Club.

her best, being flown three or even four times a day, killing the number of sixty-five rooks. Many of these flights were from tremendous slips and very high ringing ones, but never did she decline to persevere, or if beaten fail to come back from a distance, whether she could see the lure or not, to look for her master. In 1875, though at times the old dash and power displayed itself, she was hardly herself, though in a very bad season of about fifty rooks, some twenty-four were placed to her credit – and on May the 8th after a long flight down to a certain rookery – she was never seen again. It seems incredible that so sensible and well-trained an old hawk should be so completely lost – but so it was. *Rook* shooting *was* going on, but the Old Hawking Club knew nothing but the fact that they had lost a most faithful servant. It is remarkable that during the whole of her career during which she killed over one hundred and fifty rooks – *Empress* was never lost for an hour but for the last occasion. God send us more like her!

For the first time the club commenced the season (of 1876) at Amesbury, making the George Inn their headquarters, landlord, Mr Wheeler. Seven passage falcons were trained at Oakhurst, and the cadge consisted of thirteen peregrines, including *Pearl* and *Rowena* from the previous year. A start was made on 29 February, but it was very windy and nothing much was done until 2 March when *Esmeralda* flew a long and very pretty flight and killed her rook in style. This was the first time that a young falcon had killed a rook at the first time of asking, excepting *Empress*, who nobbled one in a sheep fold in her first year. During training, a passage falcon, named *Bois-le-duc*, had shown great promise and had come south from Yorkshire with a tremendous reputation. At first she would not look at a rook, refusing to consider them as suitable quarry. The weather, too, was remarkably rough and stormy and from 2 to 9 March it was 'utterly unfit for hawking'. However, on the 9th, despite it still being very bad weather with snow at intervals, *Bois-le-duc* killed a bad rook very easily. Again, for some days she refused to kill her rooks and so on the 14th she was given an easy rook, which she killed. On the 16th, although she flew a rook well in very stormy conditions, she again refused to kill it when it was sailing beneath her. The following day, again very windy, *Bois-le-duc* killed a good one, and from that day missed only one in sixty flights!

March 31st.   Stonehenge to Shrewton. Bad day's sport. No rooks out, but seven ladies out. *Rowena* killed well her second stoop. Later on would not fly at all. *Bois-le-duc* rather played at first with a good rook and let it get just too far and she did not get on terms with it till close to a big covert, where she put it in. Her first miss for seventeen flights. Later she killed a bad rook easily.

The weather continued to be stormy, but *Bois-le-duc* had now got the bit between her teeth and, whatever the weather conditions, she killed her rook every time flown.

April 11th.   Blowing a hurricane and snow storms. *Bois-le-duc* flew grand in the wind and killed twice.
April 12th.   Very windy and heavy snowstorms. *Bois-le-duc* killed three rooks with ridiculous ease.
April 17th.   Easter Monday. 6 carriages – 16 horsemen – Lovely day. *Bois-le-duc* killed three times magnificently.
April 21st.   Our party from 'The George' consisted of Messrs. Salvin, Fenwick, and the brothers Harting. All the members having gone away for a day or two, I took the command being the only member left. The day was fine, indeed the first we have had for some time without wind and rain. Had a fair day's sport. *Esmeralda* killed one rook, *Bois-le-duc* two, and *Bander-snatch* one rook and a [stone] curlew. The rook flights were easy. The curlew gave a pretty flight after a long slip. A second curlew gave a good flight but escaped by putting in. Old 'Barebones' ran away with Frost, the Falconer, and took some hurdles without leave, after which performance he came to anchor all serene. Fenwick who is clearly a right good sportsman, left by the night train.

F. H. Salvin.

Friday April 28th.   Gt. Durnford way – *Esmeralda* got her rooks well under her, made two stoops, then raked off a long way downwind and put a lot of rooks into some trees. When she came up and hustled the rooks, she knocked one down on the ground, which was picked up alive, stooped again and knocked a second rook down dead at my feet, stooped again and killed a third rook which she stuck too – *three rooks in one flight*; a second time (flown) caught very cleverly over a gorse covert, after putting into a hedge – third time caught after a rat hunt in a fold. *Bandersnatch* would not fly first time, not keen – second time caught a curlew easily – third time caught a rook second stoop. *Spinaway* and *Rowena* would not look at the rooks – neither would *Spinaway* at a curlew. Mr. Knox and Capt. Fisher out.

Despite the exceptionally bad weather, 1876 turned out the best year on record. Four hawks did all the work, with *Bois-le-duc* topping the score with sixty rooks to her credit, the more remarkable in that she did it in little more than a month, and that usually in bad weather conditions. She possessed extraordinary flying powers, was docile and of a generous temperament and tame and handy to a dead lure.

In the summer of that year eyases were hacked by Frost in Yorkshire. Two eyases were sent from a nest at Drumlarig by John Todd, one unfortunately dying soon after arrival from swallowing hay that the hamper had been lined with – the second the club had lost this way. Peter Ballantine sent two very fine tiercels, and Mr Langley a

Brailed hawks just arrived from Valkenswaard.

47

grand falcon and a tiercel. Some of these were taken to Sutherland in October, but did no good at grouse or blackcock. In that same autumn Captain Dugmore and Lord Lilford sent John Barr to Norway in order to catch some gyrfalcons, at which he was most successful, returning with ten gyrs, fifteen goshawks and several buzzards. All the gyrs but one were females and the jerkin died soon after arrival in this country. The Old Hawking Club bought two of the falcons – one a fine bird; the other, larger but not so well shaped. The latter soon developed signs of the asthma, or 'pantas', that had been so fatal to the Iceland gyrs that John Pells had trapped for the Maharajah Dhuleep Singh in 1845. The total cost of the expedition to Norway was £110 and the gyrs were caught high in the hills, considerably north of the place where Mr Newcome and the Dutch falconers trapped for the Loo Hawking Club. The gyrs were all very tame but seldom found with an empty crop, suggesting that they found their living quite easily. In appearance, they differed little from the darkest of the Icelanders, but were all dark and all immature birds.

Nine red falcons, a haggard falcon, and three red tiercels were sent over to the club by Adrian Mollen. A further six falcons, six tiercels

A haggard falcon.   *A tiercel – ready for magpies!*

48

and eight merlins were also caught at Valkenswaard that year. The sick Norway falcon died in December and the other was proving a troublesome hawk to train and on 7 January was still not nearly tame, whereas four of the passage peregrines were already flying loose by this date. On 23 December *Bois-le-duc* was taken up, splendidly moulted, and in grand condition. By 25 February all the falcons with the exception of one were thoroughly trained and all except *Juno*, the haggard falcon, had taken a rook in the foot well. The gyr was flying loose but was a great deal of trouble to manage.

The season opened on 23 March, with the old falcon, *Bois-le-duc* killing on her first outing. A few days later, one of the passage tiercels, *Aladdin*, flew brilliantly and killed his first rook. Tiercels are not often successful at rooks and were normally kept by the club for flights at magpies. By special request of a guest, out on the day, the tiercel was renamed, *Plentipotentiary* (the winner of the Derby in 1834). On 30 March, *Plenipo* – for so the name was abbreviated in the club records – flew a rook well from a long slip, caught hold, but was unfortunately badly bitten and let go. The following day, not surprisingly, the tiercel refused, and, not being taken down immediately as he ought to have been, raked off downwind to Netheravon rookery and from there nearly to Silk Hill where Newcome (Francis, son of Edward Newcome) secured him.

April 2nd. Collingbourne. *Bois-le-duc* flew twice – good flights but missed both times. *For the first time on record* a member of the O.H.C. preferred his luncheon to a fine flight by the best hawk in the possession of the Club!! Possibly the relaxation of his strictly Lenten diet, at Easter, may be held as an excuse. The case being held before Judge Wood (Standing Counsel to the O.H.C.) and Lord Chief Justice of their tribunal, the culprit was fined ONE DOZEN OF DRY CHAMPAGNE – other misdemeanours having aggravated the offence . . . for the first time we had *Freya* the gyrfalcon loose [on the down] – she behaved well.

April 12th. Met at Netheravon and hawked towards the Bustard. Flew *Beeswing* first – killed cleverly in a fold. *Bois-le-duc* put in a rook and sat down – was not keen. *Wilbury* flew well, put in, and killed. *Beeswing* put in close to The Bustard Inn, which we visited and found it let and in fair repair [the previous year it had appeared very dilapidated and unoccupied]. *Wilbury* flew well and killed in a fold. *Bois-le-duc* checked at rooks downwind and killed one a long way off. *Plenipo* put a rook well into a fold, but, frightened by the sheep, would not hunt and so missed. 7 flights.

April 20th. *Beeswing* knocked her rook a cracker 1st stoop – 2nd flight killed 1st stoop . . . *Plenipotentiary* refused to fly twice, as did *Juno* [the haggard falcon] and *Witch*.

May 2nd. . . . *Beeswing* was flown at some rooks not far from Long Barrow. She put into some premises, worked the rook out by herself, and rat hunted down a road with wattle hurdles on each side, then the rook got a start and after some fine ringing she got above it, and killed high in the air, second stoop, close to Figheldean, a very fine flight. Flew the tiercels at a magpie in a gorse near Stagg's rookery – *Cabra* fetched it well in, and *Jerry* then got in two stoops and a clever kill. Flew another magpie close to the Bustard. It got a high and long start. *Cabra* was unhooded and we had a fine piece of ringing – *Cabra* got above it, and put it into a little clump of larch, where the magpie did not dwell a minute, then some good ding dong stooping with both tiercels, and finally *Cabra* killed clever – a fine flight and fine performance on the part of the Irish tiercel.

One hundred and sixteen kills out of one hundred and ninety-four flights were the total bag at the end of the season, and would have been better had they been able to find enough rooks. The hawks, on the whole, were above the average, but not an outstanding star amongst them. Old *Bois-le-duc*, once again topped the score, killed three on the last day of the season.

May 3rd. . . *Bois-le-duc* killed a rook in good form, 2nd time killed after a hustle in a fold. 3rd time gave her a very long slip and the hawk flew a magnificent up wind flight, killing 2nd stoop, close to a large covert. We on our return home had one more try after the magpies, got them out into some bushes, and after some good flying on the part of both tiercels, *Cabra* got hold. We all left in the evening, having had a very successful season's sport.

4
THE BARNET
COMMITTEE
ESSAYS

In 1871, the Barnet Committee was set up for the purpose of developing the resources of the Alexandra Park and Palace in London, as 'a noble play-ground of some four hundred acres'. Searching for novel ideas, prizes were offered for essays to 'Illustrate the history and nature of the ancient and noble science of falconry . . . falconry, seen in its best and most legitimate shapes, will, it is hoped, add to the many attractions possessed by the Alexandra Park and Palace.' The committee – rector, doctor and esquires of New Barnet – elected three essay judges, the Rt. Hon. Lord Lilford, Edward Clough Newcome, both much respected members of the Old Hawking Club, aided by Lt-Col. Delmé Radcliffe, 88th Connaught Rangers, who had practised falconry in India.

Fisher's Essay

Charles Hawkins Fisher subscribed the winning essay with the ancient motto 'A fat hawk makes a lean horse, a tired falconer and an empty purse'. Fisher eventually published the essay in full in his own book, *Reminiscences of a Falconer*. Therein he gives many examples of what might be done in the field, and suggests:

May the aid and encouragement offered by the 'Alexandra Park' induce many an owner of English broad and open acres once more to follow the old sport of his fathers, a sport which can be best pursued in very open districts (where fox-hunting can less attain perfection), can extract the highest class of sport from partridges so wild as to be inaccessible to aught but 'driving' (not easy on downland), or the vile and paltry substitute for the noble peregrine falcon – that grotesque and unsportsmanlike imposition 'Dart's hawk-

Reverend Gage Earl Freeman, also known as 'Peregrine' of The Field.

kite, folding calico, price 9s'! And in March, when vixen foxes spoil so oft the fox-hunters' joy, can find him a capital gallop on the best turf after the fast rook-hawks a brilliant 'course in the air', if to coursing given, and a sure 'find' at no-one's expense, with no fences and few crops to be ridden over.

Moreover, Falconry, though easy enough to practise when once well-learnt, is one of those arts which, like wood turning, cannot be easily learnt from the directions of any book. . . . The sight of hoods, leashes, jesses, bells, blocks, pole-screens, etc., etc., and the hooding of the hawks, that 'stumbling block' of the beginner, accompanied by suitable explanations, under suitable restrictions, would also give a marvellous insight into the various hidden difficulties that beset a beginner in any pursuit.

Freeman's Essay

The second prize essay, with an extended title, 'On the desirability of attempting to revive the sport of falconry by its practice at Alexandra Park; and on the most effectual mode of doing so', was presented by the Revd Gage Earl Freeman, who for long had written articles on falconry for *The Field* magazine over the signature 'Peregrine'. Unlike Fisher, who clearly accepted that the idea was desirable but limited in its application, Freeman first of all questioned the advantages and disadvantages of a public exhibition of falconry and also queried whether the Alexandra Park was adapted for such an exhibition.

Now speaking in the interest of Falconry, of its public exhibition, there is something to be said for and against. In favour of it, this may be advanced,

52

that a thoroughly good thing is sure to gain by publicity. Against it, that it is impossible to see sport in perfection when bagged quarry is used, and that especially when the space is confined.[1]

As however the riding-school is the first step to a cavalry seat and not infrequently an early preparation for the hunting field, so the exhibition of Falconry in a large park may be the means of giving many thousands of people a knowledge of the way in which the sport is conducted, of inducing many to carry it out themselves, and affording to all a new and exciting entertainment.[2]

The great matter will be not to profess too much. In fact, it will be necessary for the sakes of those who look on that they should understand, how rudimentary are the lessons given and received. A great deal may be done, no doubt, with proper care and management. There will be plenty of wonder and delight expressed when a pigeon or a rabbit is chased and captured by a trained bird, which allows its master to approach it and to lift it on his glove with the quarry; but if people get the notion that the very perfection of Falconry can ever be witnessed in an English park – if they think, and tell their friends, that the sport is seen there at its best, we can only say that they are very much mistaken, very likely to mislead others, and are doing an infinity of harm to the cause itself. We would strongly recommend that these facts be thoroughly impressed upon all concerned. People are not unlikely to come to the field full of high flown notions of mediaeval falconry. Many may have heard of what is being done on the moors of Scotland and England. It is a pity if they look at what must of necessity be inferior to either of these, and go away with the impression that they have seen the real wonder of the sport. They should be told they come to see a preparation for something infinitely better, for which this may give them a taste. To see Falconry as it should be seen they must live in the wilds, or at least in the open country. They must see the peregrine falcon pass faster than an arrow over the heather with a thing that looks like a cannon ball – an old cock grouse – going downwind before her; or, better still, they must see her stoop out of the clouds with one rapid twist, as the quarry rises.

Of the suitability of Alexandra Park, Freeman wrote:

. . . all we can say is that the area is large and fairly unencumbered with plantation, while the eminence on which the palace is built will afford an excellent position for spectators. Once allowing, indeed, the desirability of a public exhibition of Falconry, it is certain that there can be not better enclosed ground selected than that which forms this great Park in the North of London.

---

1 Freeman's views on bagged quarry are shared to this day, when, quite rightly, bagged quarry is – and should be – unknown.
2 Is this a description of the first Game Fair! It is quite rightly labelled 'entertainment' rather than sport.

Dugmore's Essay

Three further essays were commended by the judges, the most unusual of which, produced under the title 'Falconry: its revival in connection with the Alexandra Park and Palace', was submitted by Captain F. Sandys Dugmore, who used the opportunity to air his views on the salary and conduct of the then Hereditary Grand Falconer of England, the tenth Duke of St Albans:

Of late years, the State Falcons – reduced to a stud of six efficient peregrines – have been at Lakenheath, in Suffolk, and in 1867, the present Duke, grudging the £200 a year which he is paid for the support of the falcons and the falconer, determined on making the office of Grand Falconer (for which be it remembered he received a salary of £1,000 a year) once more a sinecure. So the fine stud of hawks was broken up, two of the last of them coming into the possession of the writer, and crossing – one of them twice – the Atlantic with him: and the falconer – good honest old John Pells – after serving the noble house of St. Albans for 40 years, found himself suddenly reduced to a pension – or 'retaining fee', I believe it was called – of £50 a year; a beggarly pittance, quite insufficient for his support: the Duke pocketing the trifling balance of £950 a year! A fact which I recommend to the thoughtful attention of cheese-paring economists and financial reformers, who in their zeal for the British tax-payer, think nothing of depriving (in the course of their reductions) needy clerks in the public offices (perhaps with families to support) of their hard-earned £100 a year, while they allow a flagrant abuse like this to pass unchallenged! Having been absent from England, I am not aware whether anything has since been done for John Pells. I hope such may have been the case, for there are few men, if any, living to whom the lovers of hawking are so deeply indebted.

It is interesting to record that the original emolument for the Hereditary Grand Falconer, The Duke of St Albans – emolument, for no Duke receives a salary! – was a modest £391 per annum added to which a further £200 was granted each year in perpetuity for paying four assistant falconers. Besides this there was an allowance of £600 each year for the purchase of a fresh supply of falcons and hawks, a seemingly high figure when passage peregrines, as late as 1920, were only £3 10s each, although an entry charged upon the expenses of the King's household in 1399 notes the 'master falconer' expending £21. 6s. 8d. upon two 'bold falcons'.

Charles, Duke of St Albans was granted the patent as Master of the Hawk in the third year in the reign of James II, on the deaths of the then joint masters, Thomas Felton and William Chiffinch:

1691: These are to give notice, That all Deputations Granted by Thomas Felton and William Chiffinch Esquires, as Master of their Majesties Hawks in Trust for his Grace the Duke of St. Albans, are become void by his Graces being now in possession of the said Place, from where all such Deputations are to be taken for the future, in his house in the Pall-mall.

In August 1890 the emoluments to the Duke of St Albans were discussed in the House of Commons. The Hereditary Grand Falconer – more accurately, the Master of the Royal Hawks – received £965 a year, land tax and fees being deducted from the total of £1,372 10s. The Secretary to the Treasury stated 'that it was not on record when the allowances ceased to be applied to the purposes for which they were originally intended'. As a result of these discussions the sinecure was withdrawn, and commuted by the creation of a ten years' annuity of over £2,000, the total cost to the nation to be £18,335.

After a lengthy discourse on his own apprenticeship and doings in falconry, Dugmore warms to the subject of public exhibition:

Some years since, Mr. Charles Holford flew his merlins at Brighton in presence of hundreds of people – a hard pressed lark on one occasion taking refuge under a lady's crinoline. In 1867, after one month with the Champagne Club in Normandy, I took my own falcons to a much frequented English colony on the southern shores of France, and in spite of the difficulties of the country, which was full of Olive trees, managed to give a public hawking day once or twice a week, within a short distance of the town. . . . In March of the same year, the falcons of the Champagne Club and my own hawks had one or two public days' rook and rabbit hawking in the plains of Vexin.

I have now, at the risk of being charged with egotism, given some account of what has been attempted of late by individual efforts towards making Falconry popular.

. . . We have to consider, first, whether a great hawking establishment (in place of the State-supported one which has lately been sacrificed to individual stinginess) would meet with encouragement and support; and secondly, whether the Alexandra Park can be made the headquarters of such an establishment, or club, if you like the designation.

Now Captain Dugmore really gets down to his ideas, which a few years later reached fruition with the formation of the Falconry Club, of which he was to be 'The Master of Hawks'.

A good working stud of hawks, sufficient to show plenty of sport for all sorts, should consist of from six to eight peregrines, two goshawks, and eight or ten merlins. The requisite staff for their efficient management would be one professional falconer and two boys . . . The total cost of a stud, such as the above, including the falconer's salary (not under £100 a year), would be from £250 to £300 annually, exclusive, of course, of the building for their accommodation, which need not be of an expensive character. Irrespective of the extra attraction for the general public which the Park would possess in such an establishment, a considerable portion of this sum would in all probability be covered by the subscriptions of amateur falconers all over the kingdom. Many a man would gladly keep hawks, but cannot be saddled with the care of them all the year round, and has no means of providing for their management during his temporary absences from home. To such a man, the establishment of a central depot, to which he could send his hawks for a time, and where he could have them cared for by a professional during their moult, would be an inestimable benefit. Let the annual subscription (constituting membership of the 'Central Hawking Club') be fixed at a guinea a year, and let members be entitled, 1st. To have hawks trained for them by the club falconer at the cost price of their keep, plus a fee to him of £1 for a peregrine, 10s. for a merlin: 2nd. To have their hawks kept and moulted at the park at the cost price of their food (about 4d. a day for a peregrine): 3rd. To have the sole right of purchasing (by auction among themselves) the old hawks of the year when sold off in July or August, to make room for the new birds: 4th. To use the services of the club falconer in procuring untrained hawks for themselves, at a profit to him of 10 per cent on their cost: 5th. To have (if desired) the falconer and the club hawks at their own homes for from a week to a fortnight in the year (according to the number claiming the privilege), on paying travelling expenses, and boarding of the falconer and one assistant (the second assistant remaining in charge of the park), but free of all other charges.

This latter privilege would enable landed gentry in distant parts of England to enjoy a week or a fortnight's hawking over their own estates at a merely nominal cost – choice of time, would of course be decided by ballot. It would do more to establish a kind of propaganda of Falconry all over the country than could be effected by any other means, and would greatly promote the revival of the sport among all classes.

Enthusiastically, Captain Dugmore had already promoted the proposal of public exhibition to the formation of a new club, an idea eventually to create no little upset within the gentlemanly ranks of the Old Hawking Club.

5

OPPOSITION

Some few years were to pass before more was heard of the 'Central School Of Falconry' proposed by Captain Dugmore in his Alexandra Park essay. On 1 September 1877 there appeared a lengthy article in *The Field* under the title 'A Modern Hawking Stud'.[1] Readers were reminded of the efforts made by the Barnet Committee in 1871 to develop the resources of the Alexandra Park and the establishment of a 'School of Falconry'. It should be noted that it was Captain Dugmore in his essay, and not the Barnet Committee, that had proposed the idea of a school or club. *The Field* article continued:

The recollection of the efforts then made seem now to have been revived, for at the Alexandra Palace at the present time there is on view as fine a stud of hawks as one could wish to see. The stud consists of two Norwegian Jerfalcons, four Norwegian Goshawks, three French Goshawks, two Barbary Tiercels, sixteen Peregrines (seven young and nine old birds) three Hobbies, three Sparrow Hawks, and ten Merlins, besides nine Cormorants trained for fishing.

The hawks and cormorants were in the very capable hands of John Barr. The owner – 'a well-known amateur falconer' unnamed in the article, but, of course, Captain Dugmore – was permitting his falcons to be on display and to be flown to the lure to entertain the public. The article continued with a comprehensive account of the various hawks on show and their possible use in the field.

A few months later a prospectus was published:

---

1   The misuse of the word 'Stud' seems to originate from the pen of Captain Dugmore.

James Edmund Harting.

The Falconry Club

The attention of all who are interested in 'Falconry' is invited to the organiz-
ation, now in progress, of a Club having for its object the rescue from
extinction of this noble sport of our ancestors and the promotion and
extension of its practice. Visitors to the Alexandra Palace are probably
aware that for some months past there has been located in the Park, as a
loan to the Management, one of the largest establishments of trained hawks,
falcons, and cormorants in Europe.

The owner of these birds, Captain Dugmore (64th Regiment), well known
as a practical[2] falconer of twenty years standing, yielding to the solicitations
of several friends, has kindly consented, not only to allow his entire establishment (consisting of three falconers, two boys, and a large number of
hawks of all kinds, besides fishing cormorants) to be made available, within
limit, for the use of a Club, if one can be organized, but also to increase it[3]
to such a strength, and to place it on such a footing, as shall render it amply
sufficient for all purposes for which it can possibly be required.

(Since the above was penned, eighteen fine passage hawks have been
brought from Holland.).

This liberal offer on the part of Captain Dugmore has removed the great

2   On his copy of the handbill Harting crossed out 'practical' and wrote in 'would-be'.
3   Harting noted: 'too many birds already'.

58

difficulty which has hitherto stood in the way of the formation of such Hawking Clubs as have been from time to time proposed, i.e., the necessity of a very heavy outlay at starting, in getting together the necessary hawks and the professional falconers (an all but extinct race) to attend them, as well as the incurring on the part of Members of an amount of pecuniary responsibility for working expenses which few gentlemen might care to accept.

In the present instance the liability of Members will be limited to the amount of their Annual Subscriptions, as Captain Dugmore (who has consented to act as Master, with the assistance of a Deputy Master to represent him in his absence) undertakes all pecuniary liabilities, and makes good all deficiences.[4]

These conditions will place a Club in such an exceptionally favourable position at starting, that the opportunity appears to the promoters one that should not be allowed to pass; the more so, since Captain Dugmore has intimated his intention of breaking up his establishment, should the present attempt to revive the art and practice of Falconry not meet with support.

The position of Captain Dugmore as regards the Club will be similar to that of a Master of Foxhounds hunting a specified country with his own hounds and servants, assisted by a subsidiary subscription from the members of the Hunt; but, as he wishes the Club to start as free and as little hampered as possible, he does not stipulate for the collection of any particular amount; although, while he will continue for the present to provide the bulk of the required funds, the scale on which the undertaking will be carried out must, of course depend in some measure on the amount of support which the promoters are able to secure for him.

As the working of such a Club as that contemplated must necessarily be attended with considerable expense, since extra falconers and extra hawks are required to render it constantly available for all kinds of sport, it is proposed that the Annual Subscription of Members shall be Five Guineas.[5]

The election of Members will be left to a Committee of noblemen and gentlemen well-known in sporting circles.

Among the advantages to be enjoyed may be enumerated the following:

1. – Admission at all reasonable times to the Headquarters of the Club, and the Mews of the Hawks in the grounds of the Alexandra Palace (which has been selected for the present as a convenient central position), and free access to Captain Dugmore's falconers, Messrs. Joseph Mackenzie, John Barr, and Edward Gleeson, who will give practical instruction and assistance, when required, in everything connected with the management, training, and flying of hawks. Members can also have their own hawks taken care of temporarily at the Club Headquarters, on payment of a fair fixed rate for their keep.

4 On his copy of the handbill Harting has underlined this sentence heavily and has written beside it: 'an undertaking which was never fulfilled. It was left to the Hon. Sec. to make good the deficiency'.
5 Harting noted: 'Insufficient because too few members'.

Opposition!

2. – Participation in hawking parties, which will be arranged to suit the convenience of Members in any suitable localities that may be desired, such as the Isle of Thanet, for heron-hawking; Salisbury Plain, Dunstable Downs, the Berkshire Down, Aldershot and Bagshot, for rook-hawking; possibly the Curragh for magpie-hawking; and perhaps meets may also be arranged on the Continent, to suit foreign Members,[6] but this can hardly be undertaken during the first season. It is anticipated that the whole time of the falconers and hawks, during the hawking season, will be divided between such localities. While the liability of Members is, as before stated, limited to the amount of their subscriptions, it is, of course, understood that the extra expenses caused by the absence from the Central Headquarters of part of the establishment, such as travelling expenses and lodging of hawks and falconers, will be defrayed by those Members who may organize and join each particular excursion.

3. – Exceptional facilities in procuring hawks for home use. The establishment has almost unlimited resources for obtaining all kinds of hawks, and a number will be to spare every year at the close of the regular season, since only particular favourites are ever moulted by Captain Dugmore. Members will have a preferential right to obtain such spare hawks at a much lower price than would be charged to outsiders. Members can also have their servants trained as falconers at the Club Headquarters; though the resident falconers will of course expect, and be permitted to receive, a small fee for such services, involving, as they would do, much extra time and trouble. If desired, young hawks can be hacked for Members at the Master's Hawking Lodge in Ireland, which is kept for that purpose.

4. – The use, at all practical times, of Hawks for flying to the lure in the Park. Individual Members will also be permitted the use of a falconer and a few hawks or cormorants (for fishing) at their respective residences, whenever they can be spared without detriment to the interests of the Club. If sufficient support is forthcoming, the staff of falconers will be increased for this purpose, as it is thought that Members possessing grouse moors or partridge shooting may be glad to enjoy a few days' game-hawking in the proper season. A well-known Scotch falconer last season took four brace of young black game with hawks in one day.[7]

As the hawking season will commence on the 1st February, gentlemen who may be disposed to encourage the project, and join in reviving the grand old sport of 'Falconry', are invited to communicate at once with Mr. J. E. Harting, 24, Lincoln's Inn Fields, and Hanover Square Club.

So, a new club, based on the ideas expressed by Dugmore in his Barnet Committee Essay, finally emerged, with a committee composed of 'gentlemen well-known in sporting circles':

6 Harting underlined this and commented: 'Quite absurd'.
7 The Scotch falconer was Peter Ballentine.

60

Inside the hawk van.

C. R. Anderson, Esq.
Lord Clanmorris
Lord Clifton
Comte le Couteulx de Canteleu
The Earl of Darnley
Capt. H. W. Feilden
Revd Gage Earle Freeman
J. E. Harting, Esq., Hon. Sec.
Master – Captain Dugmore (64th Regiment)

The Earl of Huntingdon
Capt. A. Clark Kennedy
Tierney C. Matthews, Esq.
Burton Persse, Esq.
The Chevalier de Scherzer
Viscount Trafalgar
Lt-Col. J. M. C. Vibart, R.A.

Sixteen rules were listed. The membership was restricted to 'Gentlemen of all nations whose station, character, and position are such as would entitle them to admission to any First Class Club in the place where they reside'. A candidate for membership needed to be proposed by a member and seconded by another. An annual subscription of five guineas was payable on or before the first day of November. And every member, on election, was to sign an agreement agreeing not to employ any servant of the Master within two years of the said servant leaving his employ or being discharged, without obtaining the written permission of the Master!

The only reference to ladies in the rules, Rule 16, was quite explicit: 'Ladies proposed by Members may become Members on the nomination of the Master, or any Member of the Committee. No subscription, however, will be required or accepted from them.' Soon articles began to appear in the newspapers and magazines on the doings of the Falconry Club, and from one of them we learn that in February 1878 His Imperial Highness the Crown Prince of Austria, having heard of the new Falconry Club and wishing to see the hawks flown, visited the headquarters of the club at the Japanese village in Alexandra Park. Accompanied by Prince Esterhazy, the Chevalier de Scherzer, and other members of his suite, they were received by Captain Dugmore, Master of the Hawks, and Mr J. E. Harting, Deputy Master and Hon. Sec. of the Club. After inspecting the various hawks, the Prince 'put on a falconer's glove, and carried a beautiful tiercel named *Robin Hood*'. Carriages were made ready and His Imperial Highness then progressed to a 'meet', accompanied by the falconer and half a dozen peregrines on the cadge. Fast pigeons were provided and the Prince apparently showed great delight at the stoops made by the falcons. On their return to Alexandra Palace, a private exhibition of the tame lions were given, they then all retired for lunch. After a grand luncheon, the royal party went to the theatre to see a pantomime, and then returned by special train to town. Perhaps the pantomime was an ideal ending to such a day's entertainment!

However, two patrons were now added to club literature – His Imperial and Royal Highness the Crown Prince of Austro-Hungary and His Royal Highness the Duke of Connaught and Stratherne, KG.

The next circular to be issued to the few members that came forward was a 'Memoranda for Gentlemen Attending Meets of the Hawks':

I. – Gentlemen are requested when following the hawks to avoid as much as possible crossing cultivated ground, and to assist in preventing damage to crops and fences.
II. – Quarry to be flown at is always approached up wind, and the flight will usually go down wind: consequently the best position for spectators is down wind. If some of the field will post themselves well down wind before a flight, they may be able to render much assistance in following up.
III. – In the case of quarry taking to cover, every effort should be made to dislodge it with the least possible loss of time, if possible while the hawk is waiting on down wind, and expecting assistance: such efforts should cease if the hawk waits on very wide up wind, or appears to have given up. In magpie hawking especially, everything depends upon the exertions of the field in driving and keeping the quarry out of cover.

IV. – After a successful flight, no person must be permitted to run in upon the hawk: those first up are requested to halt at from 100 to 200 yards distance (up wind), and to assist the Falconers by keeping back all other persons, and especially dogs, which should never be brought to the hawking field.

V. – In heron hawking hard riding is necessary to save the falcons from injury: the rider first up after a successful flight should dismount at 100 yards, and approaching slowly and cautiously, kneel down and fix a cork firmly on the heron's bill, to prevent damage before the Falconer's arrival.

VI. – It may save disappointment if it be remembered that this sport is absolutely dependent upon weather, and that either windy, wet or foggy weather must render it impossible.

VII. – The Master will feel greatly obliged if gentlemen attending these meets will kindly exert their influence at all times for the protection of the hawks. Damage to game is impossible, as the game hawks are never flown in a game country without permission; and those used for herons, rooks, magpies, lapwings, and larks, are specially trained not to notice game. In case of hawks straying, information will be thankfully received by the Master, by the Head Falconer, or by the Hon. Secretary, J. E. Harting, Esq., 24, Lincoln's Inn Fields.

Added to the end of this comprehensive memorandum was the following note:

The Club subscriptions do not nearly cover the cost of the Hawking establishment and the expenses of meetings, but leave a very heavy deficit to be borne by the Master: consequently the collection of Field-money (optional) is authorized on public days. Field-money is however not expected either from members of the Falconry Club, or from Ladies who may honour the meetings with their presence.

The idea of field-money was eventually to cause much heated correspondence in the sporting papers, but the first newspaper report to incite a critical response was one in the *Marlborough Times* of 30 March 1878. After commenting on the formation of the Falconry Club at Alexandra Palace, the article noted that Mr H. Reeks, FLS, of Thruxton, on the edge of Salisbury Plain, had just been elected an honorary member of the new club. Further, it remarked that it was more than probable that the sport might at some future date be witnessed in the neighbourhood of Thruxton and the Danebury Downs, so helping in the revival of an ancient and noble sport.

Perhaps to read in a Wiltshire newspaper of the new club 'reviving falconry', while the members and secretary of the Old Hawking Club

A gyrfalcon.

were staying at a Wiltshire inn enjoying their annual campaign at rooks, was just too much. It was surprising that the Old Hawking Club had remained silent so long under the onslaught of reports and articles quoting the new club's aim to 'revive the old sport of falconry' and to 'rescue it from extinction', and so a mild but firm letter was written to the editor of the *Marlborough Times*.

64

A lanner falcon, after a watercolour by William Brodrick.

Sir, – I have read with pleasure an article in your paper of March 30th, expressing satisfaction at the so-called 'revival' of the beautiful sport of falconry by Capt. Dugmore, and at the proposed introduction of the sport into this district; speaking of it, as though hawking were a novelty in this part of the country. I therefore write to inform you that the present is the sixteenth season during which a club of gentlemen devoted to falconry have pursued this sport over the country in this neighbourhood, by the courtesy and kindness of the owners and occupiers of the land in giving them leave to do so. This club is called the 'Old Hawking Club', it has been in existence for many years, and has no connection whatever with Capt. Dugmore and the proposed new club. Its members are only too glad to see any inhabitants of this district out with their hawks, in order that they may be able to make some slight return to those who have so kindly and liberally encouraged falconry by showing sport to them and their friends. That they have been able to do so in former years their 'list of head killed' will testify.

I would therefore suggest that the term 'revival of falconry' is altogether a misnomer, and the more so, as there have never been fewer than three or four distinct hawking establishments maintained in the United Kingdom since the days when hawking was the principal sport of the country, whilst an unbroken line of professional falconers can be traced from the present day to the time when one formed a necessary part of the appanage of every large country house.

I am sir, yours truly,
Gerald Lascelles
Hon. Sec. O.H.C.
Crown Inn, Everley.

In May, too late in the season for good sport, the Falconry Club sent its hawks to Aldershot, and from there to Thruxton, and entertained the public with the occasional open day, which resulted in more letters to the papers.

Sir. – I have been informed that at an exhibition of the hawks now kept at Aldershot, and called, I believe, by the very remarkable and ambitious title of "International Hawking Club",[8] a cap was sent round to collect money in the field. I trust this report, if untrue, will be immediately contradicted, as I can conceive nothing more likely to bring discredit on the grand old sport of falconry as this unsportsmanlike proceeding.
'A Falconer of Twenty-five Years' Standing.'

[We are informed that the correct title of the club referred to is 'The Falconry Club'. We cannot say whether the report is true or not; but our correspondent seems to have overlooked the fact that the practice to which he objects is sanctioned by many sportsmen who ride with subscription packs of hounds, and is therefore not without precedent. – Ed.]

Seven days later, back came a long letter from Captain Dugmore:

8   The 'International Hawking Club' was the original name proposed for the new club but this name was thought to 'clash and interfere with that of a previously existing, most successful and admirably managed organisation, known as The "Old Hawking Club" '.

The Falconry Club.

Sir. – The animus of the letter in your last number, signed 'A Falconer of Twenty-five Years' Standing', is so very apparent that at first it seemed to me hardly worth while to notice what is evidently a mere splenetic outburst, and a gratuitous attempt to injure the infant Falconry Club from behind the save cover of an anonymous letter.

However, as you, Sir, in the exercise of your discretion, considered the attack worth printing, I suppose that I, as the Master of the Falconry Club, and myself a falconer of some twenty-two years' standing, ought (though rather against my own judgement) to treat it as worth answering. I answer accordingly.

First, it is not the case that 'a cap was sent round', or that any money was collected at the public meet referred to, or at any public meet that has taken place this season up to the present date. And had 'A Falconer etc.' wished it, or cared about such trifles as acting in good faith, it would have been perfectly easy for him to ascertain this fact before giving currency to an incorrect statement.

But, secondly, the collection of field money from non-members is authorised when the hawks of the Falconry Club are flown publicly. I should be very glad to dispense with it, as personally I cannot help disliking by precedent. . . . However . . . this field money is purely optional; so that there is nothing to prevent persons of 'A Falconer's' stamp from enjoying their sport at other people's expense, if so minded, as I doubt not such gentry would be.

Thirdly, the reason for the non-collection of field money on the occasion referred to was the failure of sport, consequent on the then falconer's [John Barr] drunkenness (even in the hawking field) and mismanagement. There have been no public days since, and consequently no field money; but the hawks have been for the last fortnight, and still are, flying daily, and flying right well, at rooks and carrion crows at Aldershot, for the private enjoyment of members of the club and their friends . . . In such an attempt we arouse of course, but despise and ignore, the jealousy and opposition of such 'Falconers of Twenty-five Years Standing' as wish selfishly to keep falconry to themselves, even though the art should die with them, and dislike – this is where the shoe really pinches – having to pay the higher prices for their fresh hawks, which are inevitably consequent on the increased demand stimulated by our proceedings. The excuse of anxiety for the interests of falconry comes ill from persons who have done, and will do, nothing to promote these interests, or any interests but their own.

An anonymous circular, which I enclose for your private perusal, and a copy of which I have handed to my solicitor, will show you what we have to put up with from persons (falconers, forsooth!) of this stamp, and to what depths they will stoop. . . .

I trust, therefore, that in case you should see fit to afford publicity to any further attacks on the Falconry Club, you will insist on, at the same time,

publishing the names of our assailants.
Master of Hawks.

Another letter in the same issue:

Sir, – With regard to the communication by 'A Falconer of Twenty-five Years' Standing' in your columns for May 11th, will you allow me to observe that I think that the said falconer ought to have signed his name?
E. Delmé Radcliffe, Lieut. Col.

The following week, 'The Falconer' returned to do battle:

Sir, – Although I have not the slightest wish to continue this correspondence in your columns, I must ask you to allow me to make a few remarks on the letter signed 'Master of Hawks', and they will be positively the last I shall offer. First, I must point out to the person who writes under this nom de plume that abuse is no argument and that if he cannot write with temper and propriety he had better not write at all; hard words, imputations of motives, and abuse will only damage his case. . . .
'A Falconer of Twenty-five Years' Standing'.

Seven days later the 'Master of Hawks' was again in print. However, a letter appeared in the same issue, pressing the various opponents to put up their swords – for the sake of the old sport.

Sir, – Permit me to echo Col. E. Delmé Radcliffes's wish, in your last number, that your correspondents on this subject should henceforth drop their 'noms de plume'. But if I had any influence with them I would beg them, in the interest of the old sport, to abstain from thus writing to you at all in future, as I am of the opinion that no good can come of it, either to our fine old sport or to themselves.
Charles Hawkins Fisher (Major)

Sadly, little notice was taken of Major Fisher's plea to refrain from making so public the unhappy disagreements between falconers. Letters continued to appear, arguing the case from all sides, but the flow was finally stemmed by a fair but firm letter from the Secretary of the Old Hawking Club again pressing would-be letter writers to keep their views out of the public eye.

Sir, – I trust you will allow me to heartily indorse Major Fisher's deprecation of the acrimonious, not to say abusive, correspondence that has been lately carried on in your paper under the heading of 'The Falconry Club'. I have read the various letters with no little amusement, but am decidedly of opinion that letters of this style must of necessity do very much to lower falconry in the eyes of such of the public as may happen to read them, and that the matter has now been carried rather too far.

Falconers cannot afford to forget that they form a very small minority among the sportsmen of this country; that their favourite pastime is carrying on a struggling and precarious existence, and that it is largely dependent upon the goodwill of many sportsmen and landowners in this country who from various causes, principally that of having never been properly 'entered' to the sport, have not perhaps a very high opinion of what they may possibly consider an obsolete amusement. Such gentlemen as these, when they read such a correspondence between a few of the small band of falconers, as that which has lately appeared in your columns, must inevitably form a somewhat mean opinion of those few persons who still patronize falconry. I feel sure that each of your correspondents has the good of the fine old sport at heart, but am equally sure that abusing one another in the newspapers is the most certain way to damage the cause they desire to promote. Whatever opinions, then, those falconers who have perhaps been trained under older-fashioned auspices to different ideas of this sport may hold, as to the comparatively recent innovations of such practices as collecting field money, of holding public exhibitions of hawks, and of even flying them at tame quarry before large crowds of spectators; and as to the effect of such performances upon the public mind, I would entreat them to keep such opinions to themselves, and not to draw attention by these heated discussions to practices which are better left to stand or fall on their own merits.

I see that several of your correspondents throw much blame on the 'Falconer of Twenty-five Years Standing' for having used a nom de plume. In my opinion, rather unjustly so, for I cannot see why he was bound to sign his name to a simple query which his first letter contained, as to the truth of a report that had long been well-known throughout the hawking world, and which had been published in at least one of your contemporaries; while the tone in which his question was answered was such as certainly to prevent his signing his name to his second letter had he been so disposed.

In apologising for occupying so much of your space, I will say that I sincerely hope I have said nothing that can possibly provoke a reply or a continuance of this unhappy discussion, and that any want of unanimity existing among the small band of falconers may in future not be so openly proclaimed to the world.

G. Lascelles, Hon. Sec. Old Hawking Club.

[This correspondence must now be closed. – Ed.]

The George Hotel · Amesbury

6
The Great Years

1877

About six miles south of Eindhoven, in North Brabant, Holland, lies the town of Valkenswaard[1], celebrated in the annals of past falconry as the home of many generations of Dutch professional falconers and as the trapping station for passaging falcons on their autumn migrations. In October 1877, James Edmund Harting, Hon. Sec. to the Falconry Club, accompanied by John Barr, club falconer, had travelled to Valkenswaard to be 'initiated into the mysteries of catching and training passage hawks', taking with them a cast of hawks in the hope of some magpie hawking.

The journey from London was not too long – by rail to Queenborough and then a nine-hour passage to Flushing; from Flushing, a four-hour journey by train to Eindhoven, travelling through flat country with few trees and plenty of water, where peewits, grey plover, ducks and herons were numerous. On nearing Eindhoven the country changed to heathland with groups of oaks and fir trees. At Eindhoven they changed carriages for Valkenswaard, where they arrived a little before midday.

Harting's description of their visit to Valkenswaard gives a good idea of how the village was in the second half of the nineteenth century:

There being no conveyance of any kind at this small and unimportant station, we engaged a porter to bring our luggage, guns, and ammunition, and carrying our hawks, started on foot for the Hotel de Valk. This hostelry has been for years the house of call for falconers from all parts of Europe, and is kept by Henri Bots, the son of a well-known professional falconer,

---

1 Valkenswaard means 'Falcon-field'. In the seventeenth century the village was called, much less romantically, Varkenswaard – 'Pig-field'.

Jean Bots, now deceased.

The house, which lies on the left hand side as you enter the village from the station, is long and low, with a screen of trees in front, from one of which depends the appropriate sign of 'a hooded falcon', We secured a comfortable sitting-room on the ground floor, with a double-bedded room opening out of it, for ourselves, and a room for our falconer; and while lunch was being prepared, we had leisure to examine our apartments. The walls were hung with pictures of hawks and falcons, which we recognised as plates from Schlegel and Wulverhorst's splendid folio work on Falconry [*Traité de Fauconnerie*], framed and glazed; while on top of a cabinet were two cases of stuffed gerfalcons, which had been preserved many years previously by the father of our host. On the left of the door in entering, and opposite our sitting room, we found a billiard and smoking room, to which one might resort should the evenings prove long or dull – an event which we did not realize. What more attractive quarters could be found under the circumstances? If the cuisine was somewhat plain, we were able to secure plenty of fish, flesh and fowl, and the extreme cleanliness of everything contributed much to our comfort. Lunch ended, we went to find lodging for our hawks, and proceeded to the house of the Dutch falconer, Mr. Adrien Mollen, who was to act as our 'guide, philosopher, and friend' during our stay at Valkenswaard. From his long experience in the capture, management, and training of hawks, we found his assistance invaluable.

James Edmund Harting.

In the palmier days of falconry, when there were as many as eighteen resident falconers at Valkenswaard, and thirty huts were put out in the season for hawk catching, he had been a pupil of Jean Bots, to whom he acted as assistant-falconer from 1833 to 1836. In 1837 he entered the service of Prince Trautmansdorff, at Oberwaldersdorf, some leagues from Vienna, where he remained until 1840, during which time he trained not only passage hawks brought from Holland, but also nestling lanners from Hungary, for flying at partridges, rooks, and thick-knees. In 1841 he became head-falconer to the Loo Hawking Club, his place at Prince Trautmansdorff's being taken by a nephew of Pell's from Valkenswaard.

The day being fine, we hardly expected to find him at home, for no doubt he would be out in the hut, hawk-catching; and so it proved. His wife, however, received us good naturedly, and we soon found ourselves in the hawk-house, a perfect model of what a hawk-house should be. On a long 'screen perch', running the entire length of the room, beneath which was a layer of fine yellow sand, sat five splendid hawks with their rufter hoods on – two fresh-caught haggards, one red tiercel, and a male and female goshawk – the last-named a beauty. The haggards were fine old birds, in the most perfect order, although not quite clean moulted, but with a freshness and bloom upon the plumage, and a bright colour in the legs and feet not seen in hawks that have been long in confinement. This bright colour is the result of high living, and a full crop daily from freshly killed and warm prey. In confinement it is not always easy to procure this; and, although there is nothing like a freshly-killed pigeon for your hawk, pigeons are dear luxuries, and can only be given now and then as a treat and a change from the ordinary diet of good lean beef.

As we gazed with admiration upon these newly-taken hawks, the beauty of whose form and colour was heightened by the new hoods, jesses, and leashes, with which they were adorned, we longed for the pencil of a Wolf to commit to paper so picturesque a sight. Our reverie was at length inter-rupted by the entrance of Mollen, who had returned from the hut – a tall, spare man, clad in a dark long-skirted coat with deep pockets, and a pair of long boots; clean shaven, with a profile that reminded us strangely of the great Duke of Wellington, and, with what Shakespeare has termed 'a hawking eye', he looked every inch a falconer. We met as old friends, although we had never seen each other before; but each had heard of the other's love of hawks, and that was quite enough to put us at once on the best of terms. He had been out since six in the morning on the look-out for passage hawks, but none had appeared, and he had returned empty-handed. The wind was in the wrong quarter, and until that changed he did not expect any luck. After seeing his hawks fed, and finding room for our own on a spare perch, we accompanied him indoors for a chat, and to arrange plans for the next day. This gave us an opportunity also of inspec-ting a small collection of stuffed birds he has, which were obtained in the neighbourhood, and preserved by one of his sons. There was nothing very rare amongst them, however; the most prized specimen being a sea-eagle, which Mollen had captured in the hawk-net with a pigeon. Amongst the marsh birds I noticed the curlew, ruff and reeve, black-tailed godwit, wood sandpiper, and spotted crake, all of which breed in the neighbouring marshes. On the chimney-piece were some half-finished hawks' hoods, the art of making which is now lost in England. Every species of hawk takes a particular size and shape, and has to be accurately fitted, to prevent injury to the eyes. Even a falcon and a tiercel of the same species require hoods of different sizes, the former bird being so much larger and stouter in all its measurements. These hoods, which are prettily made of leather, with an opening in front for the beak to pass through, and with eye pieces of green or scarlet cloth, are moulded on wooden blocks, which have previously been cut to the exact shape and size of the hawk's head; and Mollen assured us that the making of these blocks required an amount of care and skill which few would credit. The jesses and leashes are cut out of dogskin when it can be procured, and for jesses, from its strength, it should always be used; but it is difficult to get dogskin long enough for leashes, and hence calfskin, although not so good, is often substituted. The swivels and bells required to complete the hawk's furniture are both to be obtained only in Holland, no one in England understanding or undertaking the manufacture of them, and the specimens of each which may be seen here and there at our saddlers' and ironmongers' are utterly useless for the purpose. Were it not for the difficulty in procuring them, Indian bells, from their greater lightness and superior tone, are preferable even to the Dutch.

Midway between Mollen's house and the Hotel de Valk, and in the centre of the village, stands the lofty and imposing church of St. Bavon; an edifice which, from its size and grandeur, seems more adapted for a city, than for the quiet little out-of-the-way spot in which it stands. St. Bavon is the patron of falconers. . . .

Not far from the church stands an inn, known as 'The Three Swans', and kept by one Daams, the descendent of a falconer of that name. It was in the large room at this inn that an annual sale by auction of passage hawks used to take place. This was at the time to which I have referred, when there were so many resident falconers at Valkenswaard, and when strangers used regularly to resort thither in autumn for the express purpose of procuring hawks. Every owner of birds for sale was his own auctioneer. Taking a hawk on his hand, he would descant upon its age, merits, and condition, and invite bidders.

Harting and his companions enjoyed excellent magpie hawking with the falcon and tiercel they had taken with them to Holland. The country around was ideally suited for the sport, but, of course, they had to keep well clear of where the Mollens were trapping, for their own hawks would have gone to the lure pigeons. In fact, the passage of October and November in 1877 was possibly the worst on record at that time. Only seven young falcons were taken, fewer than ever known before. Very strong westerly gales prevailed throughout the time, keeping back the hawks or driving them too far to the east. Twenty-eight hawks were caught altogether, the majority at the hut at Bois-le-duc, twenty miles or so from the village. The Old Hawking Club received a total of nine hawks – five young falcons, two young tiercels (one of which was sent on to Major Fisher), a handsome young goshawk, and an adult Norwegian jerkin. This hawk was only the fourth gyr that had been caught at Valkenswaard in the memory of man, and the only one in adult plumage. The jerkin was well moulted and a beautiful bird, but with small feet. He proved to be very gentle and trained on well. The average cost for each hawk to the club was £5 12s. 0d., this including all expenses and their feeding whilst in training.

1878

By 10 February all the hawks were flying loose, including the gyr, and old *Bois-le-duc*, who had been taken up from the moult on 13 January in perfect order. The hawks left for Wiltshire on 5 March, fit from flying to the lure, and ready to enter. The weather was most unkind and for the first ten days if it wasn't blowing half a gale it was raining heavily. It was very difficult to find rooks and flights were few and far between. As Lascelles wrote, 'Rooks are without a doubt becoming far less plentiful on these downs owing to the practice of sowing "dressed", or in plain words, *poisoned* corn. Unless this practice is looked well after by the land owners both game birds and rooks are likely to be extinguished.'

It wasn't until 27 March that the haggard jerkin was given his first chance at rooks:

We then flew *Adrian*, the gyr-tiercel – a long slip at a flock; he tore away over them, made a grand ring, declining to make a poor stoop, and then came a 'cracker', the rook made for a little fence, but the tiercel had two dinging stoops before the rook put in, throwing himself straight up after each, steeple high, just like a wild merlin; he rat hunted down the fence like a magpie hawk and killed him under some sticks like a good one. It was a great triumph – the first rook as we believe ever killed by a gyr falcon[2] – the first Norwegian haggard ever caught – and after all the immense trouble

2   In fact one of the gyrs trapped by John Pells in Iceland had proved useful at partridges and rooks.

and difficulty in training him – to meet with a success the first time of asking was highly satisfactory.

March 30th. Deep snow. Crept out at four o'clock with *Wilbury* and *Adrian*. The little falcon flew well and killed after a nice little flight. The gyr flew a grand ringing flight putting into a fold and killing after a hunt by himself in grand style.

April 1st. Very cold and blew a gale in afternoon. *Adrian* never saw his rooks at all, and *Wilbury* broke a feather at starting and of course did not persevere. To finish the day while mending her feather (a very awkward break) she got loose and broke two more, while George [George Oxer, the new assistant falconer], by mistake went and fed up *Maid of Honour* for the second time today, spoiling all chance of flying her tomorrow.

After refusing his rooks for a few days, *Adrian* again killed well on 5 April, that being the last day from the club headquarters at the Crown, Everley. On the following day the club members hawked on the way to Amesbury, moving their headquarters to the George for the rest of the season. *Adrian* declined to fly.

April 9th. Very windy. Flew *Maid of Honour* first. She put in well, but did not kill. Later she killed brilliantly second stoop. *Bois-le-duc* killed after a most extraordinary flight all upwind. The old hawk making along close to the ground, gaining at every yard on the rooks and at last throwing up high over her rooks. putting them into a farm and killing. Also later on she killed one in fine style. . . . *Adrian* would not fly at all – fear he has gone amiss. One of Mr. [Percy] Wyndham's hunters out today, fell down dead while walking over a road.

A few days later, poor old *Bois-le-duc* caught a rook in a fold, where an old ewe rushed at her and knocked her head over heels, the rook escaping. This did little to upset this brave falcon, who then proceeded to kill a passaging rook from a long slip, in grand style.

Adrian was only flown twice more in the season, on each occasion going up to his rooks and then leaving them. On 25 April *Bois-le-duc* had a fit on being hooded up in the morning, and again after her first flight, which was a good one. The following morning she again had a fit, but caught a rook that day. She was not flown again that season. Indeed, in summing up the season Lascelles was to report that there was a good deal of sickness among the hawks; *Bois-le-duc*, *Adrian*, *Wilbury*, *Duchess* and *Yorkshire Relish* were all bad with various complaints, but all recovered.

That summer there was a great scrabble for eyas peregrines in Ireland, Captain Dugmore having taken all the young hawks in 1877, to the exclusion of the Irish falconers. Determined to defeat him in the summer of 1878, Mr Corbet ended in getting thirty-six eyases and Mr Hamilton eight. The Old Hawking Club could get no young eyases from Drumlarig nor Flamborough Head, but managed to get a nest of three from Horn Head in Donegal, and two eyases from John O'Groats, these all hacked by old Peter Ballantine. Two hacked tiercels were sent by Captain Hamilton, who advertised in *The Field* of 8 June 1878: 'Surplus Hawks. Nestling PEREGRINES for SALE, now flying at hack – Apply to Capt. Cole Hamilton, Birr, King's County.'

A nest of merlins, sent by Mr Pape of Newcastle, was hacked at Oakhurst, further merlins arriving in July. The club goshawk that summer was a clumsy bird, and did little except to kill a confiding merlin which came down to converse with her on the lawn. After enjoying some lark hawking with the merlins about Oakhurst, a team of club peregrines went to Middleton-on-Wolds and did quite well at partridges, three of the eyas tiercels of that year being the most successful. The disaster of that autumn was the loss of *Adrian*, on 1 October from the loft where he had been turned loose to moult. The passage at Valkenswaard was a fairly good one, but as few hawks had been ordered of Mollen he spent little time at the huts. The Old Hawking Club received eight falcons, all rather small, but a nice level lot; two red falcons came over for Major Fisher, and three tiercels, two haggard falcons and a rather nice male goshawk went to Mr Harting, Hon. Sec. of the Falconry Club. The total trapped by Mollen and his two sons was twenty-five peregrines and the one goshawk. John Barr again travelled to Norway in search of gyr falcons, this time only trapping four gyrs and a merlin. As usual, he found the gyrs very confiding. With a dead ptarmigan as a lure, Barr sometimes induced a wild gyrfalcon to follow him for a mile or more. The poor result of only four young gyrs taken was attributed to the scarcity of ptarmigan and lemming that breeding season.

At the end of the year, Lascelles sent a list of the quarry killed in the past two seasons, by the hawks of the Old Hawking Club, to *The Field* magazine:

	1877	1878
Rooks	108	107
Crows	2	6
Magpies	7	20
Partridges	37	75
Rabbits	112	6

Larks	—	29
Sundries	7	20
Total	273	263

The following week Major Fisher sent in the returns of his sport over the same period:

After reading Mr. Lascelles' account of the quarry killed by the hawks of my friends of the Old Hawking Club, and your editorial request for similar returns, I am induced to send you my own for 1877–1878.

My establishment of hawks is small, and we do not work very hard, but, such as it is, it produced the following sport:

	1877	1878
Rooks	23	56
Partridges	125	153
Fieldfare	1	—
Woodpigeon	1	—
Old female sparrowhawk	1	—
Landrails	—	4
Lark	—	1
Starling	—	1
Total	151	215

I begin and end my rook hawking in Wiltshire rather earlier than the Old Hawking Club, I believe; and, as Mr Lascelles observes, this quarry cost me also many a gallop, as well as the loss of the best eyass rook falcon I ever saw, three years old. I had plenty of partridges, good dogs and fine ground, but unfavourable weather.

C. Hawkins Fisher (Major)

1879

The winter of 1878/9 was one of the most severe ever known. A continuous frost from the end of November until the end of January, with deep snow, made it difficult to do much with the young hawks and they were all very backward. The weather gave a little about 4 February, and by the 10th the snow had gone, John Frost getting all the hawks on the wing by the 18th. Back came the snow together with hard frosts as before. Colonel Brooksbank went to Ireland, taking the club eyases with him, and George Oxer as falconer, and enjoyed some sport, returning on 1 March in time for John Frost and Oxer to travel to Everley, the ground still covered in deep snow.

Despite the weather, the club enjoyed some of the best rook hawking ever seen, with plenty of high-ringing flights. The hawks were a level lot and the score was fairly equally shared between six of the team, rather than one or two stars doing most of the work. Nevertheless, old *Bois-le-duc* produced the top score once again, many of her flights being of the highest class:

April 21st. Old *Bois-le-duc*, second time, after some magnificent ringing, the old rook made off downwind, while the falcon was engaged in making a tremendous ring. She caught him up however and killed about a mile off at second stoop, in great form – one of the best I have seen this many a day.

Towards the end of the season, usually about the first week in May, the warmer weather was a great temptation to the falcons to go on the soar and hawks were often left out. A further hazard was the appearance of young rooks in the nest, often providing an easy kill:

May 2nd. *Shooting Star* (a small neat falcon with capital style) raked off and killed a young rook at a rookery. She carried it up on to an elm and sat on a nest, eating it. A ladder, Salvin, and a long pole hustled her off at last, but she was some trouble to pick up.

May 27th. This week witnessed the break up of the Falconry Club, a split between the Master and the Secretary taking place, and the thing being found impractical to carry on. *Bois-le-duc* and *Princess* sent to Feltwell to moult. Balance sheet 1878/9 fairly favourable, showing an increased credit balance on previous year. Credits much the same; debits increased owing to one additional member! Total of year's expenditure about £280. Lord Wharncliffe failed to supply us with grouse this year, for the farmers, the Club was obliged to buy in Leeds market at an average cost of 5/6*d.* per brace. Total expenditure of £8. 4. 6*d.*

John Barr, one of the best of professional falconers and employed at different times by most of the great names in falconry, including the Old Hawking Club, died in May 1880, at the early age of forty years. Like many another good 'workman', he had one failing, which unfortunately grew on him, and led at times to reprehensible carelessness; but that one fault might be overlooked in considering how materially he assisted in maintaining the art of falconry. So James Harting, who knew him well, was to write of him in his obituary, and Barr's short engagement by the Falconry Club was mentioned with the suggestion that the club was practically dissolved at the close of the spring season of 1879. Not receiving the support which had been hoped, and the expenses far in excess of the members subscriptions, which the Hon. Secretary, Harting, had been left to make good, the club closed down and Barr was engaged by Mr Evans of Sawston in Cambridgeshire. There they enjoyed excellent rook hawking and in the autumn of 1879 went to Scotland, where they had fair sport grouse hawking.

This obituary, in *The Field* magazine, was once again to instigate a spate of long and increasingly aggressive letters from Captain Dugmore, 'The Master of the Falconry Club'. He categorically denied that the Falconry Club had been dissolved; that accepting the resignation of the Hon. Secretary did not necessitate the closing down of the club; and that Barr had remained in the club's employ until he died.

In answer came a letter from Mr Evans, John Barr's last employer:

Sir, – I have read with some surprise a letter in last week's 'Field' signed 'The Master of the Falconry Club', and, as I am the person referred to (not very courteously) as an 'outsider', I beg you will allow me to pen a few words in reply. . . . 'The Master of the Falconry Club' says that 'Barr's connection with the club was terminated only by his death, an understanding existing, in pursuance of which he took service during the past year with outsiders only while not required by any of our own members.' He does not state with whom this understanding existed. Certainly not with me, nor with Barr, who entered my service after having been for some time out of employment, and in consequence of my having advertised in 'The Field' for a falconer. Not only was I satisfied that Barr had no engagement when he came to me, but he himself several times assured me that nothing would induce him again to enter the service of 'The Master of the Falconry Club'. That gentleman next makes the extraordinary statement that he, 'was preparing at the time of Barr's death to send him out with a team of hawks, to develop an offshoot of the Falconry Club in one of our most important colonies.' No such project was ever named to me, nor to Barr as far as I know; and the idea of one man 'preparing' to send another man's servant out of the country, without first obtaining the consent of both master and servant, is really too absurd. Why I should be termed an outsider because I kept a stud of hawks without the aid of a club, I do not know. But this does not trouble me much, and under the circumstances I am content to remain
An Outsider.

Another letter from Harting followed:

. . . That the 'objects of the club have never been abandoned or lost sight of' by 'The Master' I can well understand; but that they have been long ago abandoned by everybody else I can also easily believe.

The fact is that, on the lines originally projected, the club would not and could not work, and it is much better to admit this candidly than to continue a forlorn hope.

If the club is still in existence, as alleged, why do we not hear something about it from time to time? Where are the headquarters? What hawks are there? Where were they flown during the past autumn and spring? What sport was obtained? And who are the 'thoroughly competent professional falconers' retained?

As was to be expected, Captain Dugmore was soon back at his writing desk, but the correspondence was not published. The editor of *The Field* added the following footnote to a second, rather less abusive letter from the Captain:

We have not the slightest wish to suppress any correspondence which can interest our readers, so long as it is conducted in language which one gentleman ought to use to another. This certainly was not the case with 'A Master's' letter, withheld from publication last week, which was written in a tone very different from that adopted by 'Outsider' and 'The Writer of the Article'. Ed.

So ended the letters and the Falconry Club.

1880

The rook hawking of 1880 was to be the third worst season on record. The Hon. Secretary, Gerald Lascelles, was appointed that year to the post of Deputy Surveyor of the New Forest, and removed to Lyndhurst, taking up residence in the Queen's House. With him came John Frost and his family; George Oxer, assistant falconer, stayed in Yorkshire as falconer to one of the club members, Herbert St Quintin. John Frost had married Miss Eliza Whatmough on 28 July 1875 at Hockwold Parish Church. By 1880 they had a family of three, Charles Henry (born 1876), John, and Ethel, still a baby in arms. John Frost eventually secured an old-fashioned thatched cottage at Bank and there the family were brought up surrounded by working terriers, gamecocks and New Forest ponies. Two more daughters, Alice and Gertrude, completed the family, the children going to a small private school at Gritnam kept by two elderly maiden ladies, Miss Wiltshire and Miss Oliphant. There were ten or twelve boys and girls and at playtime the whole forest was their playground.

*The Honourable Gerald Lascelles,
Secretary and Manager of the Old
Hawking Club, with a peregrine
falcon.*

Despite the poor results of the spring rook hawking in 1880, the club hawks had a successful season at partridges in Yorkshire, sadly losing old *Bois-le-duc* at Middleton early in October. Having done five years of excellent work for the club, although rather shifty in her last season, she was greatly missed, but after living out for three weeks was recovered. Soon afterwards the club gave her to the Revd W. Willimott who, living in Cornwall, a bad country for flying peregrines, kept her at semi-hack. She was unfortunately shot on a rook in March the following spring.

George Oxer at Queen's House, Lyndhurst.

John Frost.

82

1881

In November of 1880 seven red falcons, a haggard falcon and a goshawk were sent to the club by Mollen, the best of which was *Gitana*, although *Amesbury*, a very nice but small passage falcon trapped at Amesbury, was the most stylish, and produced many fine ringing flights.

26th. March. Andover Road. Nice day. Had a *very fine flight* and kill with *Amesbury*, she put into some stacks, and then the rook went away ringing to a great height. The hawk got in a fine stoop, but the rook got up again and we had some more very high ringing. The hawk then got well above and having her rook beat, killed second stoop, her first a very fine one, close to trees.

On 30 April, Salvin having brought down his trained cormorant, club members spent the morning fishing, bagging three trout and two eels.

1882

Certainly, one of the great years in the history of the Old Hawking Club was 1882. An extraordinarily mild winter enabled the hawks to be trained quickly and easily, the team consisting of eight young falcons and the two intermewed falcons, *Amesbury* and *Gitana*. A record score was put together of one hundred and eighty rooks, six crows, forty magpies (with the eyas tiercels) and three curlew, a total with a few sundries of two hundred and thirty-four head. The headquarters for the whole season was at the George, Amesbury, there being no room at the Crown at Everley during March, as the complete household of the Manor House at Everley had moved in *en masse* when the old house was burnt down. This meant many long hours in the saddle for members and falconers to reach some of the best hawking grounds.

On 5 August a team of hawks left for Invershin in Sutherland, where two club members, Herbert St Quintin and Arthur Brooksbank, had rented a small grouse moor called Achinduich. The team of hawks consisted of *Amesbury* and *Angela*, who had both been flown at rooks, *Creole*, a passage falcon from India, *Vesta* and *Virginia*, two eyas falcons of the year, taken from Culvercliff, Isle of Wight, two intermewed eyas tiercels, and *Parachute*, an eyas falcon of 1881, who had taken sixty-four head of game in that year. The outstanding results achieved in only twenty-eight flying days – one hundred brace of grouse – had probably never been equalled. *Parachute* contributed more than a quarter of the total, with fifty-seven grouse to her credit, afterwards killing seventy-six partridges in the south. *Vesta*, the eyas falcon, continued to improve throughout the season and became as near perfect a grouse hawk as one could wish. A letter from St Quintin to Gerald Lascelles on 24 August gives a good idea of the sport enjoyed.

A fine immature goshawk.

Aug. 24th. 1882

Dear Jerry,

I have not sent you a 'report' lately – I will begin by telling you that I have lost *Creole*, for good this time I fear. She went on the soar from a grand pitch on Friday, and has not been heard of. She had killed a grouse in good style earlier in the day. She was second on the list, bracketed with *Parachute*, when she was lost, so we have lost a useful hawk in her, and I am miserable for I have only two tiercels now, and one of them has the 'croaks'. We have killed 40½ brace and two hares in ten hawking days. The last three or four days have been stormy and the birds have been wild and hard to find. *Parachute* is flying grandly, quite in her old form, twice as you will see on the other side, she has killed five birds in a day. She is marvellously steady, and keeps on the wing any time almost at a splendid pitch. *Angela* is very useful, but flies in no form – *Vesta* promises well, the last two days she has gone up very well indeed, and she has a lot of pace. *Amesbury* is very slow at seeing her birds rise under her, and loses a lot of time. The birds are now able to take every advantage of a good start. We see lots of peregrines. Yesterday a young falcon followed a pigeon a few hundred yards until it put in under a poultry house right under the windows of the inn. On Tuesday I saw a tiercel knocking a grouse about (I missed seeing his stoop), and my retriever got the bird, the hawk waiting on just overhead all the time. John is bent on snaring one. Today Lady Fitzhardinge and eight other people came over from Lairg to see the hawks, but we were out. The hawking has made rather a sensation hereabouts.

Yrs,

W. H. St. Quintin

1882 Aug.	12th	14th	15th	16th	17th	18th	19th	21st	22nd	23rd
Parachute	2	2	2 1 h	1 1 h	1	2	5	2	5	3
Angela	2	2	2	2	2	2	2		3	1
Creole	1	3	1	3	1	1	—	—	—	—
A de C				1	1	1	1	very	1	1
Belfry	1				1	1		stormy		
Amesbury		1	1	2	1	2	2	and	1	1
Vesta				1	1	2	2	wet		1
Virginia									1	
Total	6	8	7	11	8	11	12	2	11	7

The grand total of quarry taken by hawks of the Old Hawking Club during 1882 was five hundred and ninety-one head, an extraordinary achievement, for which the greater credit must go to their hard-working and skilled falconer, John Frost, still a young man of twenty-eight years.

The membership of the Club had increased a little to eleven:

Lord Lilford	Col. A. Brooksbank
F. H. Salvin	F. Newcombe
W. H. St Quintin	Lord Londesbrough
B. Heywood Jones	P. Hambro Esq.
The Hon. Gerald Lascelles,	
Hon. Sec.	Hon. Members.
Falconer – John Frost	The Hon. Cecil Duncombe
	The Hon. G. R. C. Hill

Most of the members would spend the whole or part of the rook-hawking season at Everley and Amesbury. The hawks would then go to Scotland for grouse hawking, Ireland for magpies, and Yorkshire and Northampton for partridges, as organised by individual members.

1883

The rook season of 1883 did not start well, with very bad weather and the coldest March in living memory. A start was made with the old hawks on 20 March, and with better weather the young entry were soon going strongly. By the end of March thirty-eight rooks had been taken in fifty flights. The weather continued to be unsettled throughout the season – it even snowed hard on 10 May – but the season ended with a record score of two hundred and twelve rooks and crows, with magpies and sundries giving a grand total of two hundred and forty-three head. Lascelles summed up the season in a few words: 'A very good season indeed. Hawks especially handy and well trained, and the live lure unknown. One hawk was lost, and one died of "blain". Weather all through not very good and flights always hard to get.'

The grouse season was not the success of the previous year. The hawks went up to Invershin on 3 August, but the grouse were not plentiful, with very few young birds about. The eyas tiercels were not flown and the passage hawks were very disappointing. The bag, including a few blackgame, was 45½ brace. The eyas tiercels were entered to partridges and did well, helping towards a total of 43½ brace.

86

The usual lot of passage falcons were sent over from Holland and three fine tiercels for Herbert St Quintin. One of these tiercels, named *Destiny*, proved to be a remarkable performer. Trained by George Oxer, he was flown for seven seasons at a variety of quarry. he was .equally successful at 'waiting on' or at flying from the fist. He took two hundred and twenty-two head of quarry during those years, including seagulls, magpies, rooks, partridges, grouse, and pheasants.

In January 1884 His Royal Highness the Prince of Wales sent three young Icelandic gyrs to be trained by the club. Their feathers were badly broken, and two were at once sent back; the jerkin, imped with peregrine feathers was trained, but proved to be of no use.

Despite the successes of the previous year, members were curiously lacking in enthusiasm in coming down to Everley to start the season, resulting in the following entry in the club journal:

No members of the Club were willing to come down by *March 25th.*, an instance of slackness which it is hoped is now recorded for the last as well as the first time. On that date the Hon. Sec., in despair, arrived alone in order to prevent the whole season from being absolutely spent before a hawk was entered.

The mews consisted of two second-season passage falcons, seven young passage falcons, *Vesta*, the intermewed (indeed moulting) eyas falcon, two eyas tiercels, a fine haggard falcon that had been trapped on the Isle of Wight, a passage tiercel of Lord Lilford's and the jerkin belonging to the Prince of Wales. The season started badly, and on 26 March, after losing two falcons, and only catching one bad rook, the Secretary was moved to write:

Lost my knife, my luncheon, and my temper. Broke two lure strings and lamed my horse badly – what fun it is to be Hon. Sec. to a Grand Old Hawking Club!
March 27th. W. H. St Quintin came down in the morning, and G. Lascelles left.

After the first five days of the season St Quintin was to note: 'Five days hawking: 20 flights; kills, 8 rooks and 2 mags. Terribly dry and chances most difficult to find, the young hawks seem to have gone back lately, and hate the sight of rooks!'

By 2 April things were much improved. Rooks were still difficult to find but the young hawks were now going well, with three kills in three flights. However, after a rainy spell rooks began moving out onto the open down and, flights being easier to find, the sport improved. The total for the season was one hundred and fifty-four head.

1884

Two new members were elected to the club in 1884, the Duke of Portland and the Duke of St Albans, Hereditary Grand Falconer of England. The Duke of St Albans was accepted as a member upon the following conditions:

1.   That His Grace pays annually to the Club a subscription of £50.
2.   That should he require it, at any time, he shall have the exclusive use of the falconer and four hawks to be at his disposal for any reasonable time, not withstanding any other arrangement of the Club.

The second condition was never used.

Peter Ballantine, the last of the Scottish school of professional falconers, died in the evening of 9 October 1884. Lascelles had visited him in the autumn of 1877 to join him in some game hawking. They killed about five partridges a day and old Peter had a good team of hawks, in particular two tiercels, *Saddle* and his brother, *Bridle*, and a very fast bird called *The Pope*. In 1879 Gerald Lascelles wrote a short history of this fine falconer in the club journal:

. . . At Huntly Lodge their hawks were entered and used on the 12th August, and continued to fly game till late in the season, when they turned their attention to woodcock hawking, and continued to fly them right into March. This according to Peter is the finest sport which can be obtained, combining the single fine stoop of a game flight with the ringing and mounting of a heron or rook flight. At that time the woods which now clothe Deeside were young plantations; woodcocks were very plentiful and easily marked down in the open country. Peter remained five or six years at Huntly and then entered the service of Sir James Boswell of Auchinleck, where he had charge of a kennel of greyhounds, but always also trained a cast or so of hawks. He stayed with Sir James for twenty-five years, and it was during this time that he visited Amesbury in Wiltshire, to which country he gives the palm over all others for hawking.

On Sir James Boswell's death he was employed as falconer to Mr. Ewen, of Ewenfield, Ayrshire, a keen and excellent sportsman. During the time he was in this gentleman's service, Peter distinguished himself highly, by the great quantities of game he killed, and the many fine hawks he trained . . .

A female goshawk.

The best hawks he ever had were *The Imp* and *Ranting Robin*, which tiercel
he moulted ten times. On Mr. Ewen's death in 1875, Peter was employed by
Mr. Oswald, and has continued to show good sport up to the present date,
1879. The best hawks he trained for Mr. Oswald have been *Saddle* and
Pearl, which he has flown four seasons. Peter says he is eighty years old – he
walks all day and cheers his hawks with a voice like an otter hound – he has
no assistance, but that of his son by his third wife, now nine years old! And
last year he went over the cliff to take a nest. He combines all the gentleness
and clever handling of the Dutch falconers with the keenness and good

qualities of the Scotch school, is a beautiful hooder, very neat and tidy in the mews, and in all respects an excellent falconer.

Up to 1880, Peter Ballantine was almost as active as ever; at least, he could walk all day after his hawks, and cheer them when on the wing with a voice like a bell. But for the last few years nature asserted itself, and the old man failed a little, though until the day he died he had a hawk in training.

1885

Perhaps taking note of the reprimand from the Hon. Sec. in the club journal at the beginning of the previous season's rook hawking, Francis Newcome and Herbert St Quintin reported for duty at Everley on 20 March. It would be fair to add that perhaps no other member, with the exception of the Hon. Sec., was so regular an attendant throughout most of the rook-hawking season as Herbert St Quintin. A good start was made, the young falcons showing early promise, although from the start of the season the star performer was undoubtedly the haggard falcon *Sylvia*.

27th. March. Stormy. *Almida*, flown at a single rook on passage, tore away through the wind over him, and killed well after several stoops round some stacks, a rare hawk for a windy day evidently. *Sylvia* and *Nadine* – the young hawk hooded off too soon after the other, at first 'crabbed' her, and then gave up, the rooks getting a long start and going off high in the air for Beeche's Barn. But the haggard stuck to them and after a hard flight of nearly a mile, got her first stoop in, the rooks fighting hard for the rookery, and passing over all kinds of cover without putting in, finally the old hawk caught, third or fourth stoop, within ten yards of the rookery trees – a fine flight. *Sybil* and *Carmen* flew a very pretty flight for over a mile, killing at last on the edge of the Scots fir cover, the old falcon [*Sybil*] doing most of the work. *Elgiva* and *Clarissa* each got beat to cover, after dividing. *Camilla*, just before dark, killed a rook cleverly out of a flock, showing great speed. Five flights, four rooks.
31st. March. . . . Started late, as the rooks much disturbed by a lost hawk [*Lady Jane Grey*] of Major Fisher's, which we recovered for him.
April 4th.   A large field out. *Sylvia* was flown at some rooks, which reached the Everley trees before she got over them; but they did not put in, and the old hawk came in with a tremendous stoop, and killed right in the middle of the village. Second time [flown] the rook got above her after two stoops, and reached cover while she was going for a wide ring – *Camilla* killed after

Club members.

many stoops. As the hawk was killing the rook, some crows came out and attempted a rescue, actually pulling feathers out of her back, until we drove them off. *Almida*, put into premises, and then taking after a single rook that made off, killed him first stoop. *Carmen* and *Nadine* flown together, killed a rook easily. *Sybil* was flown late as she had not thrown her casting (She threw a casting on Sunday at midday containing threequarters of an inch of Ernest's[3] penknife blade, which had broken off in the head of her first rook on Friday!) she got beaten to trees for want of room. Second time she was beaten to gorse by one of four grey-crows at which she and *Camilla* were flown, the hawks dividing and the young hawk putting in some rooks at a distance. The first grey-crows any of us ever saw on the Plain. For the week – 40 flights; 32 rooks, 1 crow, 6 mags.

The season was marred by the loss of the two best hawks, *Almida* and *Sylvia*, towards the end of April, but other good hawks were in the team, a total of two hundred and eighteen head being killed that spring.

3   Ernest Kitchener, assistant falconer.

91

A hawking lunch on the Plain.

At the invitation of the new member, the Duke of Portland, the club hawks went to Langwell in Caithness for the grouse hawking in August 1885, taking seventy-one head. On returning south, a few partridges were killed at Lilford, and a good many at Scampston and Lowthorpe in Yorkshire, St Quintin's two tiercels, *Express* and *Destiny*, doing most of the work.

1886

Although a late start was made in the spring of 1886, it was indeed another great season. After the success of the haggard falcon the previous year, the new entry included two haggards, one of which, *Bacchante*, scored well, though not of the class of *Sylvia*. Towards the end of the season the weather was extremely hot:

May 2nd. Very hot, bright and dry. In the absence of the 'Gaiety Gunner,'[4] less attention than usual was paid to the Commissariat Dept., especially as regards drinkables, a matter which is *never* (in any respect)

4 'Bengy' Heywood Jones.

neglected by that gallant officer. The painful spectacle was therefore witnessed of the unfortunate Hon. Sec., alone in the midst of 'shadeless prairies', drinking *raw* 'sober-water' – faute de mieux.

A great season, with a great score of one hundred and ninety-one kills in two hundred flights in Wiltshire and a successful time at Langwell, but few partridges, it having been a bad breeding season.

1887

The hawks were sent to Everley on 10 March 1887, very backward in their training, the result of a long, hard and cold winter. On 15 March there was a tremendous fall of snow, with severe frosts which lasted until the twenty-second day of that month. Nevertheless, it was to be an excellent season, the honours evenly divided between seven of the falcons, who took two hundred and ten rooks and crows. Two tiercels, old *Destiny* and *Daniels*, a tiercel belonging to eleven-year-old Charles Frost, added thirteen magpies to the score.

May 10th. . . . Two magpies were found by the rookery, and a most serious campaign took place. First they were driven round a series of clumps and at last one went away over the down towards Druids Lodge. A long hunt with good stooping ensued, but from time to time 'Col. Brown'[5] would have his say (and suffered accordingly), and finally the tiercels were clean flown out, and Mr. Mag. left in possession of a thick bush. An adjournment for lunch was ordered which sentinel mag. watched with more suspicion than esteem. The tiercels being rested and our interiors refurbished, the fight recommenced and again, missle-thrushes, cuckoos and 'My Friend Brown' assisted this demon Pie. Finally he was driven to a single bush, and the tiercels – took to the soar! A word or two escaped the Carabineers and E.W.B.P.[6] gurgled objurgations in a waistcoat that holds many such. Yet all was not lost – Ernest went at full speed for reinforcements and returned, armed with *Marpessa*. By this time the soarers had been taken down, and one and all were launched out of the hood at poor Pie – and after a succession of brilliant stoops, *Destiny* cut short the most momentous campaign, and the career of the most artful dodger on record.

The returns for 1887 was a total of five hundred and seventy-six head of quarry, including ninety-five grouse killed at Langwell and one

5 A 'Colonel Brown', 'Mr Brown', 'Mr B' or 'Brown' was a partridge.
6 E. W. Portman.

hundred and fourteen partridges caught by *Hermes*, *Hero* and
Destiny, three tiercels belonging to Herbert St Quintin.

1888

Six passagers and one haggard falcon came from Holland in
November, all wintering well, and together with four old hawks (two
perfectly moulted by Francis Newcome at Feltwell, the others
moulted at Lyndhurst) were finally sent down to Amesbury on
23 March. Only two of the new entry showed much form, but the four
old hawks excelled themselves, again putting together an admirable
score. The old hawks were often flown in a cast with a young one to
encourage them; it sometimes went wrong.

April 14th. – *Lady Wildair* and *Seaweed* were most rashly flown at a flock
of rooks with a large number of pigeons among them. Of course the young
hawk rattled off after a pigeon down into Wilbury and was lost for a while,
and only secured by Heywood Jones after infinite trouble. . . . Last scene of
the day as we left for Lyndhurst was B.H.J.'s mare, the 'big and 'ippy
Batsay', disappearing over the skyline in the direction of the North Pole.
April 19th.   Rain all morning: could not get out until 3 p.m. Stonehenge
country. *Lady Wildair* and *Seaweed* were flown at rooks on passage, near
the Bustard. The rooks began ringing at once, and got to a great height, the
old hawk being up to them first. After five or six rattling stoops, up in the
clouds, the young hawk caught, high in the air – *The finest flight wot ever
was seen.*

Once again Langwell produced good sport, with old *Vesta* topping
the score for the sixth consecutive season, and once again the total
bag for club hawks in 1888 was over five hundred head.

1889

Membership of the club remained unchanged. 'Except for the
alterations which may have been caused by old age, loss of hair and
general deterioration of morals and otherwise', the only change in
1889 was in under-falconers, Ernest leaving to be replaced by Joe
Stone. 'Bengy' Heywood Jones returned from India in March,
bringing with him one black shahin (*F. peregrinator*) and two red
shahins (*F. babilonicus*), one of which had killed seventy ducks
during the winter (see page 112). The season started on 29 March and

by 11 May the club falcons had taken one hundred and thirty-five rooks in one hundred and seventy-nine flights, a very high average. *Squeaker*, the red shahin, did well at magpies but on the whole the club secretary summed them up as a moderate lot of hawks! One hundred and five grouse were taken at Langwell, the old passage hawk, *Elsa*, replacing the eighth-season *Vesta* at the top of the list. *Elsa*, trained in 1866, proved to be one of those rare falcons that was equally good at rook hawking flown from the fist and at waiting on patiently for grouse. In 1886 and 1887 she headed the list of rooks with forty-eight and forty-six head and in the autumn of that second year she was taken to the moors, where she showed excellent form. She continued to fly rooks for a further three seasons, and grouse another four seasons, both with great success, until lost at Langwell.

1890

1890 was to be another great year, with the results in Wiltshire beating all previous records – two hundred and forty-two rooks, and a total bag of two hundred and fifty-seven head taken in two hundred

A rook hawk on a kill.

95

and ninety-three flights. Honours were fairly evenly distributed between the falcons, *Burlesque*, a red falcon, perhaps showing more style than the others.

April 11th. Fine. Light breeze. Easton valley. *Jasmine* and *Glauca* divided, the former killing first stoop: *Glauca* flew keen but met a good ringing rook and was taken down. *Burlesque* killed cleverly, second stoop. *Ustane* (with *Matilda*) went like a shot out of a gun, and put into premises: the old hawk turned off at a downwind rook and made a good stoop, when the young one came in and killed. *Evadne* was flown at a rook in a fold which began ringing at once: she went ringing up in great form and fetched him down into a fold, but didn't care about hunting, and getting her eye on rooks downwind, went off and killed at the Rookery. *Glauca* and *Jasmine* divided, the latter going well and killing nicely: the other hawk put into bushes and went in to the kill. *Ursula* cracked over a rook first stoop. *Elsa* did the same; and *Burlesque*, going in rare form, caught high in the air, first stoop. A good day's sport. Every hawk flown, and every one except *Matilda* scoring. 8 rooks – 8 flights.

May 3rd. Collingbourne country. Large field out. *Burlesque* killed first stoop, a grand one. *Ursula* killed first stoop. *Evadne* never saw her rooks till they got too far; she put them in then went off and killed a rook at Hougoumont. *Glauca* flew a beautiful flight at a real good rook, ringing and stooping in the same place, over our heads, and killed. *Burlesque* killed easily first stoop. *Evadne* killed cleverly third stoop. *Ursula* was flown on passage, and killed after a short hustle among premises. *Glauca* killed after a hunt in a fold. *Burlesque* did the same, and *Evadne* caught another in the same place. *Glauca* put into a stack, and then changed on to another rook, which she hunted up a hedge and killed. *Ursula* picked up a rook cleverly in a fold, and *Ustane* was beaten to cover from the same field by two different rooks. 13 rooks. 14 flights.

A record day: Four young passage hawks killing 12 rooks among them, in 12 flights.

And the best flight of the season:

Ursula put into a pond, and tried to sit on him; the rook got a good start, and they went ringing up into the clouds, the hawk catching him third stoop, when they looked no bigger than sparrows. Frost said he had never seen anything caught so high up before.

On 9 August the hawks left for Langwell with their falconer, John Frost, just thirty-six years old, in charge. Despite the weather being rough and stormy, by 6 September they put together a score of ninety-five grouse: *Elsa*, thirty-one grouse; *Vesta*, eighteen grouse;

Handa, fifteen grouse; and *Ursula*, pronounced by Frost as the best game hawk he had ever trained, thirty-one grouse. Little did anyone realise that she was to be the last of so many hawks trained to such excellence, for on 17 September John Frost died at Langwell, and lies buried at Berriedale, Caithness.

The entry in the club journal is short and sincere:

On September 17th. the Club sustained the severest loss it has yet had to undergo in the death of its falconer, John Frost. He died from a heart complaint after a brief illness. He had been continuously in the service of the Club since 1872, first as under falconer, then, since autumn 1873, as head falconer. To his skill and energy most of the success and good sport recorded in these journals of the Club is due. His keenness was unfailing and caused him frequently to over-exert himself. His early death at the age of thirty-six is to some extent attributable to the manner in which he worked, never sparing himself and always anxious to show sport. His loss is very deeply regretted by every member of the Club.

7
MEMBERS

Members of the Old Hawking Club could, if they so wished, have the use of the club hawks and falconer when they were not engaged in the spring rook hawking on the Wiltshire Downs. Many campaigns were launched against the cunning magpies of Kildare and Fermoy in Ireland. It was Captain Salvin who first appreciated the potential of Ireland for magpie hawking, as early as 1855, when posted there with his regiment. Others soon joined him – including Gerald Lascelles in 1873 – and later Colonel Brooksbank and Herbert St Quintin formed a successful partnership and with their own and club hawks enjoyed excellent sport at magpies and rooks for some seasons.

Hawking in Ireland. – It may interest many of your readers to learn of the results of a hawking trip lately made to Ireland by some members of 'The Old Hawking Club'. The hawking commenced from Fisher's Hotel, near the Curragh Camp, which quarters they found good and well situated for their sport. In the management of the flights they received great assistance from neighbouring sportsmen and the officers from the camp. The Curragh is a large open space, all in grass, and consequently many excellent flights at rooks were obtained. Occasionally a wary magpie or two were tempted to come out from the enclosed country upon the open Curragh, and whenever that was the case they afforded great sport by their dodging flights amongst the furzes, into which they constantly dashed to save themselves. Many magpies were tallyhoed on and about a treacherous piece of country outside The Curragh called 'The Subaltern's Bog,' and in the long and excellent flights they gave, some of the field came to grief in crossing the wide ditches, to the great amusement of their uncharitable companions. The next scene of operations was from Sherriff's Hotel, Fermoy, Co. Cork, where the meets were large, and graced by a good sprinkling of ladies, who took the greatest interest in the sport, and crossed the country on foot in a marvellous manner. To sum up, this expedition was a great success. Indeed, the

hospitality received and the merriment and native wit which the sport produced will live long in the memory. The result of the thirteen meets were fifty-seven head killed. Viz., rooks 12; magpies 43; sundries 2.
'Highflyer' [Col. Brooksbank]

In addition to magpie hawking, St Quintin and Colonel Brooksbank had great success at grouse hawking, taking Achinduich Moor from 1882 until 1884. Some of their excellent results are mentioned in the previous chapter. For many years another member of the club, the Duke of Portland, who became a member in June 1884, although keeping no hawks of his own, invited the club hawks onto his lovely Langwell Estate, at Berriedale, for grouse hawking, to the delight of his many guests.

Herbert St Quintin also enjoyed excellent partridge hawking at Scampston in Yorkshire, and there perfected the high ringing flight at seagulls. An interesting letter recording some of his successes is well worth reading:

W.H. St Quintin.

Sir, – I have much pleasure in sending a short account of some excellent sport which I have been having this winter, flying seagulls with passage hawks and I do this the more readily in the hope that someone else may try his hand at this most difficult flight.

I first attempted this flight in the spring of 1884 and had three tiercels specially selected from those caught in Holland the previous autumn. Unfortunately flying them one day, the finest of the three, my present excellent old tiercel, *Destiny*, was badly crabbed in the wing by his companion and all chance of using him that spring was gone. We tried at gulls with an eyas but unsuccessfully.

Destiny proved useful at game, grouse, hen pheasants, partridges, magpies (at which I never saw his equal) that I neglected the gulls until the spring of last year [1889] when I again entered a red passage tiercel [*Impulse*] to fly with old *Destiny* and succeeded in killing six gulls in eleven chances with them.

On the 28th October I caught my first gull of this past season with these tiercels, and now on looking over my notes, I find that I have killed altogether forty-three gulls out of seventy-seven chances – I always count every slip as a chance, if the hawks get sighted. I had other hawks sent from Holland last autumn for the flight, and altogether entered four fresh hawks, three falcons and a tiercel, two of these I regret to say I lost – both excellent hawks, lost during the early months of the year, both lost from the same cause, viz. the hawks dividing when flown at a flock, and selecting different gulls. If there is any wind blowing when this occurs there is a great risk of losing one or both hawks, as from what I have seen of the flight it is almost impossible for the hawks to kill a common or black-headed gull unassisted under several miles unless it is done at the first stoop.

To show what risk there is I may say that, besides losing these two hawks on three occasions this winter, I have had hawks out at night from this cause. And yet we always have two field glasses out and have taken every precaution to avoid such a thing happening in hooding off. One day the tiercels divided, and one of them was picked up on a gull over five miles downwind of the place where he was hooded off. I believe the gull killed to be one at which he was flying when last seen. This tiercel had a habit of always taking the highest and furthest gull if flown at a flock. We finally lost him one day going after gulls which turned downwind high in the air, and I never heard of him again. With this red hawk, *Jehu*, and my tiercel, *Impulse* (in his second year), on the 11th. January last we caught a Herring Gull out of a small flock after some pretty stooping. The gull which I have had mounted, is all but in adult plumage, and I think the little hawk's performance is worth recording. Four of the herring gulls were caught with falcons after short flights, and there is no doubt that with properly entered falcons they are more easily caught than either of the other two species, being much slower in shifting from the stoop. Falcons seem to be more easily entered to gulls, but my tiercels, though their feeding

Seagull hawking.

naturally requires more care, and they are certainly *not* fond of gulls, have shown more brilliant flights – nothing that I have seen approaches the style of *Old Destiny* and *Impulse* when slipped at a single gull on passage, perhaps not even directly upwind as they should be. *Impulse* rattles away the first, rapidly mounting higher and higher, while *Destiny* skims along the ground until he gets nearly up to the gull when he suddenly runs up almost perpendicularly, as if drawn by a string, and goes over him ready to stoop. If, as sometimes happens in a long slip, the gull turns round in the wind in front of the hawks *Impulse* shoots himself up forty or fifty yards into the wind above the gull then turns over and puts in a downwind stoop which fetches the gull nearly to the ground. *Destiny* in the meanwhile has been going higher and higher when, seeing the gull brought beneath him by the other tiercel, he comes down with one of his terrible zigzag stoops, sometimes landing on the back of the gull tho' the latter more often shifting quietly avoids him and perhaps we have thirty or forty stoops and some pretty ringing before he is accounted for, or the tiercels are defeated by the persistent shifting. Good as their condition is from hard flying and careful feeding, in such country as this, which is too much enclosed for good rook hawking, it is a great thing to have a quarry which never 'puts in' unless it be into water, the neighbourhood of which must be avoided. Most of these gulls were killed about fifteen miles inland from the sea, and I should say that five out of six were flown on passage, sometimes at very long slips.

		Gulls:
Janette	passage falcon.	
Inbrette	passage falcon.	Herring gulls 5.
Jasmine	passage falcon.	Black-headed gulls 10.
Jehu	passage tiercel.	Common gulls 34.
Impulse	intermewed passage tiercel.	
Destiny	intermewed passage tiercel.	

Score: 49 gulls in 88 chances, between 28th. Oct. and 15th. March.

For the first few seasons Herbert St Quintin thought it necessary to use passage hawks only; indeed, after his first successes at common gulls he seemed to think that the black-headed gull might prove too difficult to take.

March 19th. '89.

Dear Jerry, – I have just achieved a great success with the tiercels. They had not had a chance since Friday until this morning, when we drove out to a likely place on the wolds. It was a nice dull morning with a hard cold breeze. As we went along, we saw a flock of ten gulls on a fallow, and got down and slipped at them. The young hawk (*Impulse*), fetched them in, and made a good stoop, and then another. The old fellow (*Destiny*), went hard and high, and we saw him apparently wait for the young hawk's second stoop, and then came down splendidly right on the gull's back, and the young hawk joined him nicely on the ground. We fed the hawks on a pigeon, and pocketed the gull, a fine old bird (Common gull) in adult plumage. About an hour afterwards saw two or three more hunting over a field. As they seemed to be moving away we took one on passage, rather high, and not quite in the wind, but the tiercels rattled off and fetched him down well. The young one got first stoop, then the old one, and then the young one caught him nicely by stooping straight downwards on to his back. We then fed them up on warm pigeon, and let the gull go. I dare say falcons might enter more readily, but I think there is no doubt that tiercels can kill gulls, when they go hard and mean business. If we meet the little black-headed gulls some day, we shall see if the hawks can account for them. I almost doubt it.

Yours truly

W. H. St Quintin

As has already been noted, the tiercels managed black-headed gulls very nicely, although undoubtedly they were the most difficult to catch. Eyases, too, proved well suited to the sport, St Quintin commonly flying a cast of an eyas and a passager together.

Jan. 6th. 1897. Could find no gulls. Gave it up and were driving home, when a small flock of gulls settled in front of us close to the road. We trotted past and got downwind, and slipped out of the dog-cart with the tiercels. *Rocket* (passage tiercel) went through the wind at a great pace, and was over the gulls directly and trussed a very large bird in immature plumage [herring gull]. *Saracen* (eyas tiercel) put in four good stoops at another gull, but was beaten.

Jan. 14th. Wet snow showers, but wind light. Found lots of gulls on Knapton Brow and near Winteringham. Flew *Rocket* and the new passage tiercel, *Starlight*, in a good place and *Rocket* fetched one well. The young one was going straight and high and I thought he was in a good position to catch, but unluckily he stooped at the old hawk instead of the quarry and the old fellow would not fly any more but sat in a tree. Took them down. Later, on Knapton Brow a common gull coming past low and upwind, we decided to take him. Moody [falconer] hooded off *Saracen*, and the little eyas went well. It was the first time that we had given him the lead, and I was rather doubtful if he could fetch the quarry as the wind was at that moment blowing fresh. But there was never any doubt as soon as *Saracen* got sighted, for he began, as usual, to go high over his quarry, and soon got a good stoop in, followed by another which brought the gull near us and I thought the falcon might go. She got sighted at once, and went well, and soon was stooping, stoop for stoop, with the tiercel. *Syren* [young passage falcon] got rather excited and soon began to course [stern chase] and the tiercel did too, and I thought the gull would get the better of them. Indeed he did once get above both hawks, but luckily they each went for a ring and fetched him down again and flew him very keenly down the line of a fence, the falcon at last, to our great delight, getting hold. She behaved very nicely on the ground with the tiercel, and has certainly an excellent temper. Seeing gulls below us, we left the hill, we came upon a flock on a grass field close to the village. *Rocket* went for the furthest gull and fetched one, but others came back under the young hawk and he turned over and picked one up which I believe was watching the other hawk, for it never seemed to see *Starlight* until too late. However we were delighted to get him blooded on his own gull. *Rocket* seeing what had happened left his gull, and joined in on the ground. Two new gull hawks entered.

Another club member who spent the greater part of the rook hawking season on duty at Everley and Amesbury was 'Bengy' Heywood Jones, who joined the club in April 1882. One of four brothers, known to their friends as Oliver, 'The Boss', 'Bengy' and 'Wengy', and all equally famous as polo players, Bengy has left some interesting notes in his diary of hawking and hunting in India, during the years 1884-9.

Feb. 6th. 1884.   Got to Bombay. Looked round the Arab dealer's stables in the afternoon.

Feb. 7th.   Bought a grey Arab pony, 'Wizard'.

21st.   The Rapore bird-catchers brought in a passage saker falcon, which they said would catch kites. Flew her at a kite on the native Cavalry Maidan, but there were so many about she was bothered and did nothing.

23rd.   The Rapore men brought the saker again. Flew her at a kite outside the R.H.A. lines. She rang up prettily with him but left him to stoop at another kite which came along below her and caught it.

March 3rd.   Good hunt at a jungle cat in the public gardens with the terriers and secured him.

6th.   The wild geese made such a clatter in the early morning they woke us. No boatman turned up to work the ferry-boat. Had to pole ourselves across. Shot 8½ couple of snipe, and one teal. Rode back to Sialkote.

18th.   The bird-catchers brought in a haggard red shahin falcon; four feathers in each wing and her decks not moulted.

May 4th. Sunday.   Quail shooting 22½ brace.

18th. Sunday.   Beat the pig covert by the river for pig. Only had twenty beaters, and couldn't get them away.

25th. Sunday.   Lots of pig, but could not shift them. One beater got cut over and the rest funked.

July 1st.   Two falconers, Futteh Khan and Mom Khan, arrived.

July 23rd.   Took out the merlins and killed a mynah bird down by the racket court.

Aug. 3rd.   Flew *Sudder* (eyas lagger falcon) for the first time at a paddy bird, which she declined. The paddy bird is a little white heron, about as big as a Norfolk plover. He don't fly very fast, but is a beggar to put into any sort of cover, water for choice. A sort of aquatic magpie, but a good deal faster.

13th.   *Sudder* mopped up a bad paddy bird easily. *Pinktail* (sister to *Sudder*), put another down twice into a pond, and then into trees. Got him out with great difficulty, into another pond, and out of that into more trees. Here she raked off at some tame ducks, and I gathered the paddy bird with a clod of earth.

19th.   *Pinktail* had a good flight. They crossed the nullah, which was full up, and put into the sick lines. I had to leave my pony and swim, and I couldn't hustle him fast enough on foot. She got disgusted, raked away and was lost. Looked for her until dark.

20th.   Mom Khan picked up *Pinktail*.

Sept. 17th.   Hawking, Khotli way. The haggard laggar *Sukey* raked away from the lure and killed a crow. Had a lot of trouble with her. *Pinktail* flew badly and ought to have killed. A new laggar that I bought that day put a paddy bird into a well, and we got him.

19th.   Large field of women out hawking, consequently disasters. *Sukey* got beaten to covert by a crow. Flew *Sudder* and *Sukey* together at a crow,

A saker with 'sealed' eyes, having just been trapped.

which beat them to cover, and *Sukey* played the fool and took us the rest of the evening to get her.

21st. Sunday. Marched out to Beni Singh, on the Chenab river, and camped there.

22nd. Crossed the river and put up at the Dak bungalow at Phuklian. Phuklian is, I think, the most sporting place I ever was at. There are plenty of geese, duck and snipe; not in the great numbers in which you see them further south, but enough for hawking. Lots of jackals to hunt, but before the sugar cane is cut, the coverts are so enormous that they take a lot of catching. The same applies to the pig, of which there are a few about. Lots of jumping, but one or two of the big drains were too wide, at least for our horses. Plenty of masheer in the Chenab river: the biggest I ever saw killed was 53 lbs., killed by Sir Michael Biddulph at Beni Singh. We lived in a little three-roomed bungalow, and we built a rough kennel for our fox hounds.

26th. Killed a fox with the terriers in the morning. *Pinktail* wouldn't try. *Sukey* killed a crow very cleverly among a lot of small trees. *Gitana* put into a khet and I caught the paddy bird. She then killed another, first stoop.

Oct. 10th. *Gitana* killed a paddy bird after a hunt round a pond. *Sukey* killed a bad crow that did nothing but dodge about my pony's legs. Flew her again on the Native Cavalry Parade ground, and she got beaten to the lines

A native falconer with two peregrines.

by a good crow. However she picked up another by the Guard Room.

19th.   Sunday. A little shahin falcon and a peregrine tiercel came in from Pindee. Ali Shah brought in a fresh caught passage peregrine falcon.

26th.   (On duty) *Sukey* killed a crow behind the lines. She afterwards flew a fine flight, and killed him behind the Butts. *Gitana* had a long hustle at a crow, but knocked herself out of time by flying against Michael Cradock's pony's legs, and of course failed to kill.

27th.   Futteh Khan went out on his own with the new shahin to look for duck, and promptly lost her.

31st.   Stephen Biddulph came with his hawks.

Nov. 6th.   Bought a fresh-caught peregrine tiercel. 3 rupees.

7th.   The fox hounds arrived.

12th.   Ayat Khan, who was out looking for *Sukey* (lost on 7th.) picked up a haggard laggar with jesses and a leash on, which he found on a crow she had killed.

17th.   Desperate hunt with the terriers at a big wild cat, they got him.

18th.   Turned out a jackal by the Wazirabad road for the hounds. Ran him for an hour and a quarter, and had to stop them at dark. Hounds naturally short of condition.

23rd.   Hawking at Rungpore. Flew one of the tiercels at a peewit, and lost him. *Gitana* killed a crow.

24th.   Futteh Khan brought in *Sukey*. Bought a haggard red shahin from him. 5 rupees.

29th.   Sir Michael invited us all to a pig-sticking meet at Agra Chuk (in Kashmir territory). Saw plenty of pig, including one whacker, but couldn't get them out (of cover). Killed a brace of teal with Stephen's shahins.

Dec. 21st.   Hawking. The peregrine falcon *Kitty*, killed a heron. *Gitana* a paddy bird.

29th.   Hawking. *Kitty* caught a black curlew, and fell with him into the

An Indian falconer, with guest and goshawk.

river, but never let go. Futteh Khan had to swim in and rescue her. *Cox* (tiercel) killed a peewit.

Jan. 2nd.   Met at the Cat covert. Away at once, and ran past Shangton Holt best pace up the river. A five mile point, first half fast. Hawking. *Kitty* flew a grand high ringing flight at a curlew. They got up a fair height before she saw them; but she went up a great pace making enormous rings. She fetched them high, hit one hard twice, and caught him near the ground. A fine flight. Just after this we came on some villagers who said they had some pig hidden up in a khet. Sent back for spears, and joined in at once. Owen and I were on one side, and a small boar came our way, and we got him. Then found Cradock with a big boar in the garden, being badgered by men and dogs. Several of the men had enormous spears, as big as spades, and the pig came out and charged one of these warriors close to me. The nigger brought his weapon down to the charge and stood like a hero, and next minute he and the spear went flying about 40 feet, but he got up none the worse. However the pig left at once, and Cradock got well away with him. As luck would have it they met at the big drain, and pig, Cradock and his pony, Master of Arts, all went in together in a heap. Pig out first, but Cradock, who had never parted company with his pony, was a good second, and overhauled the pig in the next field, taking a good spear off him. He then turned to fight, and I got up in time to get in an ineffectual spear, and help to slay him. A good big boar.

18th.   On duty. Futteh Khan took the hawks out and caught a black stork with *Kitty* and two peewits with *Box*.

22nd. *Box* flew a grand flight. They went up so high that even in the Indian winter evening, as clear as gin, they were both out of sight, and we could only now and then catch the flash of the white underwing of the peewit, when he shifted from the stoop. At last he gave up, and dropped headlong into a big pond, the tiercel cutting sideways at him all the way down. Went in and retrieved him, as he could fly no more. This is the best flight I ever had the luck to see, and we only saw the half of it. *Kitty* hit a heron hard, but then left it.

25th. *Kitty* was driven away by a wild falcon and lost.

28th. Rode out to Phuklian. The river was bankfull from the heavy rain, and we had an awful job to get over, having to ride our ponies shoulder deep into the river, and jump them into the boat. Our food and kits didn't get in till 10 p.m.

Feb. 8th Pigsticking at Deaspore. Got eight pig.

Score for 1884–1885 Hawking season.
37 paddy birds, 40 crows, 3 cattle egrets, 28 peewits, 1 heron, 4 jays, 2 various. **Total** – 123 head.

August 11th. 1885. Bought two young laggars, *Ada* and *Elfrida*.

Sept. 5th. Marched out to Mari. Cradock, Owen, Stephen and I. No sort of road! Had to lead our ponies most of the way down a boulder strewn bed of a dry mountain stream. They lost all their shoes and were all lame.

6th. Drove the nullah for Chukor partridge. Beautiful shooting, but awfully difficult, as it was like the side of a house, and they came over you downhill like bullets, while it took all your time to stand up to shoot. Got 7½ brace, 1 quail, 1 green pigeon and one beater damaged by Stephen.

Oct. 22nd. Our hounds arrived from Murree.

Nov. 9th. A shahin and a young peregrine came in from Hazroo.

14th. Put the new shahin up over duck, but at once a wild peregrine came at her, and drove her clean away. Bad luck.

22nd. Out after geese with Owen, three geese and a crane. Fished the rest of the day. The General had elephants with him, and generally fished from out of the howdah.

23rd. Marched into Jummoo, with Sir Michael and Owen. Fished all afternoon. Got five among us. In the evening we all dined at the palace with the Maharajah. Went there in state on a very swell elephant, with two regiments as escort. The whole of the female population of Jummoo out on the roofs to see us. We were shown the Maharajah's swell reception room, full of cuckoo clocks, musical boxes, and cheap French Prints.

Dec. 30th. The peregrine falcon waited on well over duck at Kotli and caught one, but fell into the water with it, and let go.

Jan. 5th. Stephen [Biddulph] arrived with his hawks; two old shahins, *Lohi* and *Burduck*; a young peregrine falcon, and a young tiercel. Took them out and killed a curlew with the falcon, and a peewit with the tiercel.

7th. Hawking at Palial. *Lohi* and *Burduck* each killed a duck in their usual finished style. Noor Khan's falcon killed a gadwal. My tiercel was put up over teal, but raked off, and killed a starling. Stephen's falcon had a good flight at a heron, but there was too much water about, and he put in a long way off and beat her. She afterwards flew a beautiful flight at a curlew, and killed him in a khet. His tiercel also killed a teal after a long rat hunt.

12th. Palial. *Lohi* killed a duck at the big jheel. *Burduck* and my shahin, *Eliza*, killed a teal, after a desperate hunt. Flew both tiercels at a peewit, and killed after some nice ringing. On the way home Stephen's tiercel, who had been fed, killed another peewit, with his crop full! The falcon killed a curlew near Waterloo.

30th. The falcon killed a gadwal in the brook, clever. The saker flew well at curlews, but put into a khet, and would not have anything further to do with it. The tiercel put a peewit into a khet, and I caught it and threw it to him. But he stooped so hard at it, that he hit a clod of earth, sat down on the peewit, and just quietly died.

Feb. 11th. Pigsticking at Deaspore. Before the beat began, Gordon and I, who were together, saw an old boar making back, and laid on to him at once. I was first up on 'Wizzard', when he cut sideways at me. I only got a bad spear into him, and he sheared off, but was in again at me before I was expecting him. I very nearly missed him altogether, but just managed to drop the spear into the very top of his withers, and he dropped as dead as a stone. The spear was whipped out of my hand, and the whole head and shank twisted up like a fish hook. One of Wilkinson's best spear heads!!

18th. Left for England.

Score for 1885–1886 Hawking season
6 curlews, 10 paddy birds, 9 peewits, 25 ducks, 5 crows, 5 various.
Total – 60 head.

October 8th. 1888. Arrived Bombay.

17th. Arrived at Meerut, and put up with Stephen Biddulph. Found he had got a nice lot of hawks for me.

27th. The young falcon, *Morgiana*, caught October 4th., made fifteen stoops to the lure. Bought a nice young peregrine for twenty rupees.

28th. Went out early with Stephen's old falcon, and killed an egret. Two more fresh caught falcons brought in. One a very big one. Bought her for fifteen rupees. Stephen took the other at fourteen rps.

We now have the following hawks: 3 old peregrines, 6 young peregrines, 2 young peregrine tiercels, one old shahin, *Squeaker*, one young shahin and two shikras.

Nov. 1st. Arrived at Chichawatni, the nearest station to Jhung. Sixty miles, and a bad road, desert and sand all the way; didn't look much like hawking country. Had a tonga and relays of ponies. Dined and slept at the Dak bungalow. From the roof of this bungalow you saw a perfectly clear

Stephen Biddulph with Morgiana.

Native falconers with goshawks, sakers and peregrines.

horizon line all around you, just like being at sea, without a tree in sight.
Nov. 3rd.   Jhung. Jhung must have been a biggish station at one time, as there were many bungalows going into ruins. In the afternoon some wild-looking ruffians turned up with a female and two male goshawks. Killed a crow in the garden with one of them later. The Nawab Amir Khan came to call in state, with a lot of ragged followers carrying hawks of sorts. He was a delightful old gentleman, who had blown every penny he could get hold of, and he signed on to come with me, and show me the way about, and find us

something to hawk. He was as keen as mustard, and used to gallop his old screws about, regardless of the consequences. We had a desperate hunt at a fox in the garden with two of the Baron's mongrels, but he beat us.

5th.   The young falcon bought Oct. 27th., *Miss Pinto*, comes ten yards to the lure.

8th.   Have got two falcons ready to fly, but no 'houbara' [McQueen's bustard] to be got. Went out with the Nawab and killed seven grey partridges, three black partridges and a hare with the goshawks. This is a great country for short winged hawks; everybody seems to have a sparrow hawk if he can't afford a goshawk.

10th.   March to Shahjewahl. Sandy desert with jahl bushes. Lots of cranes and sandgrouse, but nothing else. Fine hawking country but nothing to fly at. *Miss Pinto* comes one hundred yards to the lure.

19th.   Crossed the Jhelum. Houbara tracks all about the camp.

21st.   Found a houbara and flew *Mrs. A.* and *Mrs. B. Blood* nailed him. Everybody much excited, and yelling like maniacs.

23rd.   The young falcons had a long flight at a houbara. I had no idea a houbara could go so fast.

Dec. 1st.   The old falcon met a good houbara which flew bang away from her. The Nawab's goshawks killed a brace of partridges.

10th.   Flew the tiercels at a peewit, which *Buz* caught, while the other tiercel cut over a gadwal. Flew the shahin at a peewit, but she raked away at a parrot. However she came back and killed the same peewit. *Mrs. Blood* had a long slip at a houbara, and caught it on the ground, but got kicked off, and wouldn't try any more. A pair of laggars came up and hunted her out of sight. The Nawab found her just before dark, all smothered with the houbara's excreta,[1] so no wonder she was sulky. She was bright green all over, and we had an awful job washing her.

11th.   I found that the only way to get at houbara in jungly country was to put the falconers on camels, and then to follow the freshest tracks we saw. Being so high up, they could generally spot houbara some way off, and they were not shy of camels.

22nd.   Out round the jail, and flew *Buz* at a peewit, which he hunted right into the jail, where we couldn't find it. It was a long way round to get in, and we found a prisoner of sorts had hold of the hawk: doubtless the peewit was secured for the pot. Thank God the hawk wasn't!

Jan. 7th.   Good day's hawking. Later shot a peacock by my tent. I should have got into a row over this if anyone had split on me. There were lots of them about round the villages, and pretty tame, but the villagers hated you shooting them, and there were strict orders against it. However we managed to get a young pea chick for the larder now and then, and very good they were.

---

1   A regular form of defence with the houbara. The oily excreta are similar to bird lime, and on a falcon's wings make it difficult for her to fly. They can be removed with hot water.

31st.   *Buz* killed a peewit in a khet. *Huz* flew a fine flight at another and caught in the water. In the hunt I nearly fell over a fair-sized crocodile, but didn't get a chance at him with the gun.

Feb. 7th.   In the afternoon we flew the Rajah's hawk at the local flamingoes. They had been there all winter, two pairs of them, and they were quite tame. They were a source of endless argument among the falconers, who had never seen anything like them before. The hawk unluckily took on the old cock, who went a good pace, but she put him down into the water a long way off, and we couldn't get up in time to help her. Flew her and *Mrs. Blood* at curlew, but a flock of bar-headed geese got right up in front of them, and she stooped at and caught one. The hawk and goose went rolling over and over in the mud, and another goose stood over them and whacked them with its wings. We only just got up in time to secure the goose.

16th.   Jummun came back from Hazroo with two shahins, a black one that went to Lord Lilford, and a red one which went to W. H. St. Quintin.[2]

18th.   Cut both the tiercels loose. They went at once and bathed in a puddle on the high road, and sat on a garden wall to dry. I was afraid some loafer would pick them up, and we couldn't scare them away. Gave the old hawk to Stephen. I wish now that I had brought her home.

Score killed by my own hawks, and three lent by Stephen Biddulph.
Mrs. Blood 8 houbara, 1 curlew.   9.
Mrs. Atchinson 5 ducks. (lost)   5.
Old Falcon 5 houbara, 42 ducks, 15 teal, 1 var.   63.
Miss Davis 1 houbara (given away)   1.
Shahin 12 peewits (lost)   12.
Huz 22 peewits, 7 jays, 1 various.   30
Buz 2 teal, 36 peewits.   38
Jack 5 jays.   5.
Squeaker 27 ducks, 15 teal.   42
White Lady 3 ducks, 16 teal.   19
Total   228

Stephen Biddulph's hawks caught an additional 23 ducks, 20 teal, 1 bar-headed goose, 1 white necked stork, 7 egrets, 11 black curlew, 24 herons, 2 peewits and 5 various. **Total – 94 head. Giving a grand total**   322 head.

   In the season 1890–91, the old falcon that Heywood Jones gave to Biddulph killed:
16 houbara, 21 ruddy shelducks, 78 ducks and teal, 1 merganser, 1 smew, 4 bitterns, 11 coots, 1 lesser cormorant, 1 darter, 1 stone curlew, 1 Himalayan berbet, 1 Indian crow. **Total 137 head.**

2   See page 94. *Squeaker* was also brought to the United Kingdom, was successfully flown at grouse, partridge and magpies, and lived until 1891.

John Anderson, falconer to Malcolm Fleming, on the occasion
of the Coronation of George IV, July 1827.

(*Above*)
*A painting by Gilpin of a peregrine, belonging to Colonel
Thomas Thornton, killing a ptarmigan.*

(*Right*)
Comet, *an intermewed eyas tiercel, from a painting
by William Brodrick.*

Glauca, *an intermewed passage peregrine, from a painting
by G. E. Lodge.*

*A peregrine on a grouse, from a watercolour by an
unknown artist.*

A peregrine with eyases, from a watercolour by an unknown artist.

A Greenland falcon at Het Loo, Holland, from a painting by Joseph Wolf.

Shark, *an adult male goshawk, from a painting by
William Brodrick.*

An immature Barbary tiercel, painted by William Brodrick and given to Charles Hawkins Fisher, who had given the hawk to the artist.

Falcons on a pole perch.

A falconer with a fine goshawk.

113

The great variety of quarry available, the more predictable weather, and hawks of many different species so cheaply and easily obtained gave many officer/falconers great opportunity to pursue the sport in India. Indeed falcons were almost too easy to obtain resulting in the following comments from Lt.-Col. Delmé Radcliffe:

I broke [trained] five falcons and four tiercels; but lost a tiercel and caught a falcon immediately after, and I let the young shahin go. Since I arrived at Delhi, I caught a young tiercel and two falcons, and I had one falcon brought to me. Magnificent hawks! but what on earth to do with them I don't know. One peregrine was taken from the train of the rebel Begum of Oude. She is two years old, and has not a blemish; very bright blue, with a bloom on it, and a fast hawk. My best falcon, *Tigress*, is an old falcon which I caught myself at Bijnow. She had moulted clean before she was caught and is a very black hawk. Falconers are in the habit of saying the young hawks are the fastest, but this is surely impossible. Undoubtedly old hawks are much the more difficult to manage at first. A young falcon is the next best: she is capital at black curlew; and I have frequently seen her take the long-billed curlew. This she would do, turning from a heron in the most provoking manner. She is nearly as fast as the old hawk. I have two clipping tiercels; splendid plover hawks: it is a capital sport, plover hawking! none but passage hawks, I am sure, could do it.

My falcons are flying at herons, white herons, black curlew, wild ducks, spoonbills, and one has killed a crane. The tiercels fly white herons, teal, plover, and paddy birds.

. . . I saw a curious thing near Billore lately. A young falcon of mine had flown a black curlew. She killed close to some natives, unfortunately in the edge of a river. She was at this time rather shy, having only just completed her training. The crops were high, and there was no open space large enough to call her to the lure, she eventually sitting on the bank, on the far side, near to where she had cut the curlew down into the water. I was preparing a pigeon on a long string so that she might catch it in the air, when five or six wild geese came over, high in the air, and passed over the falcon. To my horror, I saw the falcon look up, open her wings, and rattle away after the geese as hard as she could go. 'They won't stop under six miles,' said my falconer. He was mistaken. They went until they were specks in the sky, and I had given up hopes, when the specks looked larger and larger – so we all said. There was soon not much doubt the geese were returning, but the falcon was not to be seen. At last they got within easy sight of us, when all of a sudden the geese opened out in all directions, and the falcon shot like an arrow through them, marking her course with a cloud of white feathers, leaving one goose staggering, while the others made the best of their way off. The falcon was up again in a few seconds, and at him again, with the same result as before. At the third attack she bound to him, and fell about two hundred yards on the other side of the river. One of the Nawab's

114

falconers swam over and lay by the falcon. I galloped off to a bridge about a mile off, as I did not want to get wet under a hot sun with ten miles to ride afterwards, and came up before the falcon had done feeding, most fortunately, as she would not let the naked falconer get within ten yards of her, but jumped off the goose. That was the most extraordinary flight, and the luckiest, I ever saw. I let two magnificent old falcons go last night. One of the falcons instantly killed a parroquet, the other rattled away after some teal, over the Jumna, at a great distance off.

But let us return to Francis Salvin, for so long a member of the Old Hawking Club. He inherited Sutton Place, Guildford, through his mother's family, but, being a confirmed bachelor and finding Sutton Place too large, for most of his life he resided at Whitmoor House close by. Every season would see him involved in the excitement of the rook hawking on the plain with peregrines, but he was a great enthusiast of the goshawk, of which he trained many fine examples. Salvin also introduced fishing with trained cormorants and otters. In 1847 a member of the Loo Hawking Club brought Salvin a cormorant from Holland, which he eventually succeeded in training. The cormorant became a most successful fisher, and was aptly named *Isaac Walton*. In the summer of 1849, Salvin made a tour in the northern counties with four trained cormorants, taking one thousand two hundred fish in twenty-eight days. He often took them with him to Amesbury, to provide variety to the sport, and fine fish for breakfast, and in 1888 took them with him when rook hawking with Thomas Mann on the Essex–Cambridge borders.

April 13th.   Went to Ickleton. Captain Salvin with us with his Cormorants, we began our day's sport by fishing at Ickleton Mill Stream. The Cormorants fishing well, killing some very fine roach and a pike.
April 17th.   Went to Chesterford. Took Cormorants with us and fished at the Mill (Mr. King's). The Cormorants taking six or seven fine roach.

On another occasion, on the River Whalfe, the cormorants took forty-five fine trout in seven hours' fishing.

Nicknamed 'the Arch Imposter', by his fellow club members, Salvin not only kept cormorants and flew his goshawks in the long passageways in his large home, to keep them fit in windy weather; but he also kept a wild boar as a pet and for many years had a pet monkey named Jumbo, who, wearing a red jacket, would ride across country mounted on a large brown retriever.

115

8

The Crown Inn. Everley.

TWENTY-FIVE YEARS

Fortunately for the Old Hawking Club, George Oxer was able to take over the post of head falconer on the early death of John Frost, and remained with the club for twenty-five years.

The passage hawks of 1890 were brought over from Holland by Paul Mollen, brother of Adrian, and falconer to Lord Lilford. They were trained at Scampston in Yorkshire, the home of Herbert St Quintin, as Oxer remained in St Quintin's service until December of that year. Young Charles Frost, the eldest of John's two boys, who had been assisting his father as falconer's boy during the previous two seasons, replaced Oxer at Scampston, although only fourteen years old.

The winter was the coldest recorded since 1813, with very hard frosts as early as November and heavy snowstorms starting about Christmas. On 15 March a terrific snowstorm with huge drifts closed the whole country to traffic and up until the beginning of April there was hardly a fit day on which to get the rook hawks out. It proved a moderate season for sport, although one hundred and forty-six rooks were taken, which was well up to average. One of the old hawks, *Ursula*, was responsible for a third of the rooks killed, the young hawks being a fair lot, but not getting enough flying to bring them on. There was not a single day of warm rain to bring the rooks well out onto the down, and flights were very hard to come by.

George Oxer had done very well in his first season as head falconer to the club. He had been trained by John Frost and in 1877 was assistant to him, employed by the Old Hawking Club. Although he later became falconer to Herbert St Quintin, he rarely missed the rook hawking in Wiltshire, went magpie hawking in Ireland on many occasions, joined forces with John Frost for grouse hawking at Invershin, and produced first-class sport for his master in Yorkshire at

116

George Oxer, falconer to the Old Hawking Club for twenty-five years.

partridges and seagulls. Thanks to the skills taught him by Frost, and his natural understanding of hawks and their ways, George Oxer – 'Uncle George' to many friends and children – was well able to maintain the high standards set by his predecessor, and season after season, whatever the weather, the annual results gave evidence of his success. Every autumn, George would travel out to Valkenswaard to collect and train the fresh-caught falcons supplied to the club by Mollen, and returning to Lyndhurst would finish their education in time for the annual migration to Everley. In the summer he would be responsible for hacking any eyases and training them in time to entrain for the north for the Glorious Twelth, and then perhaps to Northamptonshire, Lancashire, and later Wiltshire for a campaign at partridges. The club falconers with their long green coats, silver buttons embossed with the letters OHC, were much travelled and made friends in many places.

Over the years, many falcons were trained by Oxer, both passagers and eyases, and in most years there would be one or two that would outshine the others in performance. All too often the best hawks are lost and in 1892 *Swiftsure*, a passage falcon showing the most perfect style and way of going, was repeatedly lost, recovered and finally lost

117

The 'hack' house. A snare is set to capture the hawk on the feeding block.

Eight young peregrines just taken up after five weeks at hack.

for good. She contributed only twelve rooks in a total score of one hundred and twenty-nine. That same year, at Langwell, a Dover falcon, *Agatha*, turned out a real good one, but was also lost in the enclosed country about Lilford at the end of September.

The following season, two first-class passagers were trained – *Midget*, the smallest of the young entry, and *Danceaway*, a large powerful falcon. *Midget* showed excellent form from the very beginning, but *Danceaway* was a slow starter and not at all clever with her feet at the beginning of the season. However, she finished with a score of sixty rooks, killing three on the last day, probably young rooks of the year, which provided little sport.

May 12th. Last day. Blowing from the west. Up Nine Mile Water. The day may be summed up by *Danceaway* being flown thrice, and *Midget* twice, all at, as it turned out, bad rooks, all being caught easily. Five flights, five kills. A bloody day – a rotten day – but just not – a b — — y rotten day.

'Let it be remembered that this makes the twenty-first season since the present Hon. Secretary took charge of the affairs of the Club.' So wrote the Hon. Gerald Lascelles at the start of the 1894 season, a season again dominated by *Danceaway*. She had been moulted, along with *Midget*, at Larkhill, Lancashire, the home of Heywood Jones. It was the practice to put the falcons out to moult with various members of the club. Newcome invariably moulted at least one each season at Feltwell, where hawks had been kept for over a hundred years. This plan made it easier to feed the moulting falcons, as much as possible, on natural food.

In the summer of 1895, Adrian Mollen died and the hawks for that season were caught by his son Karl. It had been Adrian Mollen's practice to handle the fresh-taken hawks while his sons were out at the huts and to 'break them to the hood' once they had learnt to take a good crop of beef through the hood. Without his father's help Karl did not have the time to do this and all the hawks that were earliest caught were left on the pole perch in their rufter hoods all day, instead of being taken in hand. This resulted in many of the hawks that year being bad jumpers, restless in the hood.

A couple of the young falcons turned out very well, yet once again old *Danceaway* was not only top in the list, with fifty kills to her credit, but also produced the best flights of the season. James Harting, now a member of the club, came down from the city to enjoy the sport:

'*Shall we fly the young falcon?*'

'*Let's try* Black Lady.'

120

Unhooding the falcon.

The falcon on her kill.

April 4th. 1896   Left London by 9 a.m. train from Waterloo and got to Collingbourne at 11.45. Found a trap waiting for me and learnt that the hawks were coming to Hougemont, en route for Easton Valley, and that I should likely meet them. I rode out in search of them and very soon saw the van and made out Lascelles, Heywood Jones, Fowler, and a visitor, Hussey Freke, from Enford . . . We went over a lot of ground without finding any rooks and at length sighted some in the distance on a fresh fallow. Got well up and slipped *Danceaway* and *Tailley*;[1] both flew well and the rook gave them a very short flight, and was cut over at the second stoop. Another long tramp before any rooks could be found and then in an awkward place to get at them. A hedgerow too near them downwind, but no better chance offering. *Ivette* and *Winifred* were hooded off, the former chased her rook down into a valley, but did not kill and was taken down by Heywood Jones. The latter singled out a rook, but on going for it, an unlucky partridge got up and was instantly killed and carried half a mile to a gorse covered hill, where the hawk eventually alighted and was taken up by Fowler whose horse on being left, bolted, and galloped away to a farm where I recovered it, and brought it back to him.

A capital season, with *Danceaway*, once again, taking the highest number of rooks.

In the autumn of 1896 some club members took a partridge manor at Enford. The weather was bad and birds scarce, but a young tiercel, *Siegfried*, proved to be the very best partridge tiercel yet owned by the Old Hawking Club, killing fifty brace. He was unfortunately lost at Lyndhurst in the winter and shot by a lout at Brockenhurst. That winter the club was to lose its principal supporter and long-time member, Lord Lilford.

Osra came over in the winter of 1896, with five other passage falcons, a haggard, and a passage tiercel. In training she came on well and on the first day of the season killed a rook 'like a professional'.

March 23rd. 1897.   Beautiful day . . . *Osra* flew magnificently at a big flock, going high over them, and making several feints before she singled one out, when she had three or four splendid stoops at him: but had to go for a ring, then caught him first stoop. A very fine performance. . . .
April 2nd.   Fine day, cold in the morning, nice mild evening: showers all round us but we kept dry. *Osra* caught second stoop, but came down such a bump that she let go, and had to ring to recover him. Flown again she caught first stoop. *Danceaway* had a long slip at a flock: they got up very

1   The name was not *Tailley*, but *Trilby*. Harting probably misunderstood Oxer when noting the names of the hawks.

Casting off . . .

high, but the old heroine kept driving on, letting rook after rook pass under her, till she fetched the very highest of the lot into a stack, and killed unassisted.

April 22nd. The Bustard. Fine: strong N.E. wind. Large field out, 12 horsemen and women out at one time . . . *Osra*, as usual, took the very furthest rook from a very long slip, and killed in grand form, second stoop. Flown again she mopped up a crow in a gorse. Third time she put into a fold in the Tilshead valley, and had a longish hunt, the rook apparently dead beat but she let him get over her, had to ring, and only got in two rattling stoops before he got into Tilshead village. She hunted him right through the village and out the other side, where she had to ring again, and he finally beat her down wind to the rookery beyond. Such determined hunting was never seen before by the writer of these notes.

Danceaway had a very long slip, and did not see her rooks at first: they got a good start and beat her to covert, though she flew her very best and got in two rattling stoops. Flown again, at another very long slip, she never got a stoop, but was beaten upwind to covert: went on the soar near Tilshead and was lost. . . .

April 23rd. Blowing very hard from N.E. Out towards Tilshead, but at the Bustard met young John Frost [second son of John Frost, and assistant falconer to Oxer] and W. [Billy] Coleman, who had got *Danceaway* at about 9 a.m.

Osra had set a new record with a total of seventy rooks scored to her, beating the record of sixty-five rooks taken by *Empress* as far back as 1872.

A capital season's sport was enjoyed in 1899 but marred by the death of two good hawks:

Lucifer, *a young eyas tiercel, from Dover, 1899.*

Blaine with the passage tiercel Ready.

Ready *at one year old, 1899.*

124

Billy Coleman with hawks on the cadge.

Black Lady *on a partridge, 1898.*

*Partridge hawking. Blaine is behind the cadge in a straw hat,
with Best, his falconer, to his left and, to his right, Radclyffe,
holding the spaniel.*

April 26th. . . . *Minette* went right well over a good rook on passage, and
put in two grand stoops before he got to the rookery near the Bustard. We
were anxious to kill with her and hunted a long time; at last she made a
dashing stoop right down to the ground, through the trees, just missed her
rook and killed herself, *stone-dead*, against a tree, a sad, sad sight. And so
home, very sad at thinking on poor *Minette*. No such accident having ever
been recorded in the Club annals.

What a day, for the following entry appears in the club journal for 26
April:

April 26th.   This morning was brought in the dead body of poor old
Danceaway: she was found in a dying state in Wilbury Belt by a labourer
on the evening of the 23rd. (having been lost on the 18th.) and died next
day, evidently shot.

Danceaway

This famous old hawk deserves a line in memoriam. She was first trained in
1893 and a very big dashing black falcon she was, with a ravenous appetite.
When in best form she generally ate the best of two rooks a day. Her style
was most brilliant. She could race up over rooks with hardly an effort, but

when there would never make a bad stoop, but frequently made false ones, missing the rook by a yard or more, and terrifying it most ably, but often not meaning to kill it until her sixth or seventh stoop. She appeared to stoop for sheer love of it, not always to kill, but when nearing covert, or if the rook got an advantage, her stoop was very difficult to elude. With this style of flying, she was the perfection of a hawk to show sport though perhaps not the most deadly rook killer that we have possessed. Her temper was perfection, and she was always as tame and gentle as a cat. She killed in her first season no less than sixty rooks – as under:

1893. 60 rooks.	1897. 38 rooks.
1894. 54 rooks.	1898. 25 rooks.
1895. 49 rooks.	1899. 12 rooks. (to April 18th.)
1896. 50 rooks.	**Total** – 288 rooks

Her average for her first four seasons was fifty-three, and this is a record unapproached by any other rook hawk. It is not too much to say that up to the middle of the fourth season she never did wrong, but after that time she began to grow rather cunning and after an unsuccessful flight was rather inclined to rake away, and seek for a rook for herself. Latterly, the habit became confirmed and she would disregard the lure altogther, but generally kill a rook in sight. When she did not she was lost for a few days and though she never got in the least bit wild, yet she stayed out once too often and a miscreant with a gun did to death the best falcon of modern times.

With the dawn of the twentieth century, the club continued to thrive. Membership remained steady, at about nineteen or twenty, but with changes as some of the founder members and older members retired or passed away. The Revd William Newcome died in 1897, having lived through and enjoyed sport with three different clubs, from days at Didlington with the Falconer's Club and the Loo Hawking Club, and the last of the heron hawking with his brother, to the annual rook hawking with the Old Hawking Club. But other changes were to come – to the country over which the club had hawked for so many seasons. Barbed wire had made its appearance some years before, and had been the cause of some unprintable comments in the club journal, but that was nothing compared to what was to come.

April 16th. 1900.   Easter Monday. Gale of wind, with showers and bright intervals. Too rough to fly. Rode across the downs to Amesbury, past miles of new Rifle Butts and Camps. On arriving at Bulford were horrified at the sight of a brand new full scale Railway, running past Tanner's Gorse to Amesbury!

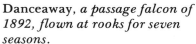

Danceaway, *a passage falcon of 1892, flown at rooks for seven seasons.*

The falcon Dover *at two years old.*

Despite the awful growth of army camps and ranges which restricted the amount of suitable ground, the club continued to start the season from the Crown at Everley, and to move their headquarters to the George at Amesbury in the middle of April. Each autumn, George Oxer would travel to Valkenswaard to collect the new hawks, and in 1901 trained a haggard falcon, *Shelagh*, who proved to be as good as any the club had owned. Haggards, in contrast to passage (immature) falcons, are usually unreliable, difficult to keep to their legitimate quarry, and easily lost, knowing well how to look after themselves. Few are therefore worth the trouble of training. But occasionally one is caught that lends itself well to being trained and, if they take to the quarry entered at, can show a skill in flying and manoeuvring that even few passage hawks can accomplish. *Shelagh* took a total of fifty-four rooks in her first season, and sixty-two in 1902, in both years heading the list with her successes. The magpies, which had featured but little in the sport of recent years, again in 1901 created much hard riding and much more hard swearing, two passage tiercels belonging to Gilbert Blaine helping to add to the score, and further sport was guaranteed by 'The Rat and Badger Club'.

May 5th.   The Rat and Badger Club proceeded by Route March to Prospect Farm, where they killed forty-seven rats among the old Bully-beef tins, left lying about by the Army.

Most of the members brought their favourite terriers with them; nor were fighting cocks unknown to both falconers and members of the Club.

'In May, 1902, the Hon. Cecil Duncombe, Senior Member and founder of the Old Hawking Club, died, to the deep distress of all his many friends.' Cecil Duncombe had outlived by six months his fellow falconer, Major Charles Hawkins Fisher, who, in the spring of 1863, had joined forces with him to enjoy rook hawking from the Bustard Inn on Salisbury Plain. Hawkins Fisher, a close friend of all in the club, continued to maintain his own team of rook hawks, spending each spring at his hawking lodge at Chitteme, and working that side of the plain. The club, as we have seen, would make its headquarters at Everley and Amesbury. Further members joined the club, including Charles Garnett of Great House, near Chippenham, who remained a

On the lawn, Church House, Shrewton.

stalwart until a year before the club's end, and Sir George Noble. Sir George Noble was initiated into the mysteries of the sport in 1891, and acquired a goshawk from France. It unfortunately escaped and was soon shot, though for a long time after it was dead Sir George used to get claims from farmers claiming she had killed their prize poultry. That autumn Sir George wrote to Mollen, and two passage falcons were ordered, one of which turned out particularly well considering the inexperience of the falconer. Named *Elsa*, she killed a great deal of game, including a curlew – a great performance.

On 1 April 1902 the club moved to the George at Amesbury for what was to prove the last time. The country around there was now so cramped, and spoilt by army camps, that more and more time was spent hawking around Tilshead and Shrewton, and later in that year the Hon. Secretary purchased Church House, Shrewton, as club headquarters.

The 'Hawkers' farewell to Amesbury.
Dedicated (without permission) to B. Jones Esq. 1903.

Many have sung how Life is full of parting and of pain,
And now my simple lay must help to swell the sad refrain,
How happy days, and golden hours must soon or late be past,
How all good things must have an end, and time is flying fast:
For us the World is out of joint, and things have gone askew,
And now as exiles we must roam, and seek for pastures new.
Oh! black and evil was the day, ill-fated was the hour
When on this pleasant land was cast the eye of Martial power.

Its barbarous hand swept farms away, and where God's work was fair
Unsightly huts and hideous butts, it quickly planted there.
The 'Bible', where some 'Hawksters' keen have ridden from the brow
Scowls down upon a hideous town, of tin-roofed buildings now.
Where 'Laodamia's' flying feet, have cut the springy sod
And *Danceaway* in cowering rooks has 'put the fear of God',
The sunny Downs, the Valleys green, we knew and loved so well,
Are covered now with Notice Boards, and scarred with bursting shell.
Gone are the buildings, where for lunch we've sheltered many a time
And studied, scrawled upon the wall the Yokel's homely rhyme.
But the plantation still exists, where sat the aged wight
Sheltered among the trees that put a finish to a flight.
Who called us all 'Hard-hearted Dogs', and though we did not beg
Later, in gratitude for Alms, he showed us his bad leg.

Amesbury farewell! No longer may the Hawking Club resort

130

To their head quarters at the 'George', in search of fun, and sport;
No more shall Van, and men in green wander adown the street
No more to old Sandell's shop, meander 'Benjy's' feet.
Alas! For us all this is changed, those pleasant days are fled,
The Shop has passed to alien hands, the 'Fell-monger' is dead!
No more from the familiar stall that held his ancient bones,
Shall honest 'Stinker' in the morn come pottering o'er the stones,
No more beside the old stone bridge, deep in his favourite pool
Shall 'Silver Penny' take his stand, his fevered legs to cool.
No more at night with appetites sharpened beyond belief
Shall we devour the doubtful fish, the mutton and the beef.
And watch with admiration deep, 'Benjy' devoid of fear
(Or conscious of cast-iron guts) swallow old 'Hussey's' beer.
While Members new, and favoured guests, listen to tales of yore
The Secretary can produce from his unfailing store.
(His stories of the 'Bustard' days, when all the world was young
Of doings of the O.H.C. had better not be sung)
And 'Sefton' (Club contortionist) will do his level best
To put all others off their food, though eating his with zest.
All that is past – the fun, the sport, the famous flights we've seen
And pleasant memories only, now remain of what has been.
The morning's ratting, then the start, all eager for the fray,
The varying fortunes with the Rooks until the close of day.
The mad joy of the Magpie hunts, when drawing 'Tanner's Gorse'
Or 'Porton Firs', with frantic noise we screamed till we were hoarse.
Till cracking whips and hideous cries no longer might be stood
And 'mid loud shouts of 'Gone away', 'Mag' left the sheltering wood.
While 'Benjy's' curses, loud and deep, and his blood-curdling yell,
Consigned all others than himself to lowest depth of hell.
Then driven on from bush to bush, hustled from tree to tree,
Pursued by Tiercels, men and noise, what earthly chance had she?
So some might think, but through it all quite cool is 'Margaret's' head
She never is so much alive, as when you think she's dead.

*   *   *

But if of all we've done and seen I should attempt to write
I should not end this doggrel rhyme, though I sat up all night.
'Tis useless now for us to waste our time in vain regret,
And though we sadly say 'Good bye' yet we shall not forget,
What sport we've had, the records of the O.H.C. can tell.
Let's hope for pleasant days to come, and 'Amesbury' fare thee well!

As Charles Garnett had noted in his diary for 1902, *Shelagh* had
undoubtedly been the best of the falcons that year in style and

Haggard falcon on block.

everything and, having moulted well, much was expected of her in the spring of 1903. She started well by killing seven rooks in her first eight flights, but was then lost: 'An irreparable loss. She was getting cute and preferred a flock, but her style was undeniable.'

April 14th. Club moved to Church House, Shrewton (from Everley). Some difficulty was experienced by the remount Dept. in getting over the downs and the horses were six hours and more in getting across the plain . . . Rode down to Shrewton and unpacked.

Out from the new headquarters at Shrewton, and on to new ground previously used by Major Fisher, the club enjoyed excellent sport, and a young falcon, *Josephine*, became a new star to replace the lost *Shelagh*.

May 30th. A nasty day, drizzling rain most of the day. S. wind, fresh. Spent most of our time in a stable venturing out when it faired a bit to fly at some very handy ploughs [rooks following the ploughs]. Tilshead. *Josephine* flown at a flock, selected the furthest and killed first stoop. Flown again she hustled round some ploughs and killed easy. But her third flight, was the flight of the century!! . . .

Flown at three rooks on passage, she put one of them, a very small teg [young female] rook, little bigger than a jackdaw, into some trees. After a short hunt he began ringing and they went up real high, the hawk ringing grandly and fetching him down into Farm buildings with a rattle, after a couple of tremendous stoops. Here she had to hunt him again, and after getting scraped, he went up ringing again. Again they got up high and again she fetched him into a small clump. He wanted no hunting this time but left as soon as we got up, and started up ringing again; but the pace was beginning to tell on him, and she did not let him get up very high. However he made his point, and just struggled into the Covert on the hill S. of Tilshead, with the loss of most of his tail, fetched in with three very vicious stoops. She hung over the covert, although any number of rooks were about in front of her, and kept her eye on the hunted rook. B.H.J. tried to take her down to his dead lure, but she wouldn't look at it. Finally H. Talbot rode into the covert and cracked his whip, and the hawk being rather wide, the hunted rook slipped off downwind for Tilshead Rookery. Round she came and after him hard all the way, running into him close to Tilshead Lodge, the best part of three miles from where she was flown. Four hunts, and three different sets of rings. The best flight I have ever seen. . . .

May 8th. Fresh wind from S.E. Out towards Tilshead and home via Ellbarrow and Shrewton Folly. *Josephine*, near West Down, put in with three nice stoops, to some trees - a desperate hunt ensued from one tree to another, and up and down an old hedge, killing at last. The hunt lasted

J. Allen with the falcon **Black Lady**.

J. Allen with a young falcon and tiercel.

134

about ten minutes. *Brenda* in a nice place, killed first stoop. *Josephine*, slipped in a good place, but nearly downwind, killed with a brilliant second stoop, a long way off – as was to be expected. *Josephine*, next flight, put into a fold and after a hunt, drove two away and put them into a strongish clump of trees. Here a terrific hunt ensued, lasting many minutes. The blasting was terrific, The Chasseur d'Afrique [Mr Hussey Freke] was more than usually active and comminatory beyond measure. No God-fearing rook dare to remain in any wood with such explosive forces at work. At last the rook left and *Josephine*, who had made many brilliant cuts at him, nailed him at once. But the Chasseur drew a long breath and continued to emit execrations – of horrible character – for some time after the rook was dead – and he had to be kindly assured that there was no more need for his strenuous exertions!

The following season *Josephine* again made the highest number of kills but was very nearly lost on 9 April when she went after downwind rooks, unseen by George Oxer, when he slipped the falcon at her proper rooks upwind. She turned down wind in a moment and was gone. Luckily Heywood Jones rode for his life after her and all was well.

Josephine continued to do well in her third season at rooks, 1905, but two of the seven passagers trained that year turned out particularly well. One of these, *Aimwell*, was to set a new record of seventy-two rooks to her own foot. Although the club started operations at Everley in the time-honoured way, the country there was also being heavily fenced and planted with woodland, and so the hawks went to Shrewton almost immediately. Charles Garnett, one of the most enthusiastic of members, having rented the Oliphants' house in the village, enjoyed a comfortable season with many guests adding gaiety to the party. So many women present led to the following comment:

The advent of so many women produced much coffee-housing, and at the time of writing the evil consequences are not capable of being accurately gauged. Many more hawkers came out this season. G. Blaine is a new recruit and a welcome one, knowing the game and keeping hawks of his own. . . . A fine lot of hawks this year. We have more than we require. *Old Josephine*, among the patriarchs, taking pride of place. She is not quite so good as of yore, being more knowing, but can and does show how the thing should be properly done now and again. *Brenda* and *Rosemary* (two second season falcons) helped to make the young ones. The young ones are a very unusually good lot. *Aimwell* is quite remarkable in pace and style, and is already one of the best hawks, if not the best, the Club has ever owned. She will take on anything, and also hunt when required. May she live as long as

An immature gyrfalcon belonging to Blaine.

Old Danceaway. Margot in any ordinary year would be notable. Lacking *Aimwell*s style, she is a powerful flyer and a wonderful footer, frequently killing with a brilliant uppercut to which she is very partial. . . . Owing to these three good hawks, the others have not had much trial.

Gilbert Blaine's two passage falcons, trained that year and flown with the club hawks, were very different. *Scylla*, a small dark falcon, was very gentle and tame and proved to be a good magpie hawk. The other falcon, *Charybdis*, was a good second-rate rook hawk. She was a light-coloured falcon, shy and difficult to hood, and a jumper when hooded. This falcon was very fast up to her rooks, and a beautiful stooper, but often did not drive them home and was always chucking it. She was handicapped by having three feathers imped in each wing. Gilbert Blaine also had a very fine wild-caught Greenland gyrfalcon in immature plumage which he had bought from Cross of Liverpool for £8. Although in perfect order and tame, she arrived with a stiff wing and could never be flown.

The year 1905 certainly turned out to be a year to remember, many of the flights being of the highest class:

April 29th.   Moderate wind but squally. Rooks not very far out.
Aimwell, at an easy flock, put in one fine stoop and cut out her rook, but then played with him, not going up, though keeping control, and killed fifth stoop easily. Flown again, at a side wind slip, and she flew strong and putting her rook into a fold, killed cleverly, unassisted.

136

Margot, at a cross wind slip, flew very finely, fetching her flock down wind, and cutting out her rook first stoop, killing him high up second stoop. A very fine performance. Flown again later she killed an easy rook before we got on our horses. She twice showed an inclination to carry.

Josephine, at a fold above Middle Barn, kept control well, flying high and putting in several stoops with great dash. At last she raked away rather far and the rook was off for Middle Barn, where after a very short hunt, aided by labourers, she killed him. Flown again later she gave an exhibition of rook hawking as it should be done. At a long slip upwind, with a flock, she went straight into the wind, mounting very fast. Now at a great height, she put in one stoop and cut out her rook. Promptly throwing herself downwind after him she made a big ring, and coming high over him killed a good rook with a magnificent stoop about two or three hundred feet up. A very brilliant performance.

May 8th. *Aimwell*, at a long slip, went up fast as usual, and killed first stoop. Again, she took on a distant rook, not the one intended, but proved right, never changing and killing first stoop. Long slips make no difference to her. . . . I consider it a very good season, and as far as we were concerned, a most enjoyable one. The weather was not very good, cold and rather windy as a rule. Rooks were, to my mind, distinctly stronger than usual, and we had more than the usual number of ringing flights, in spite of good hawks.

That autumn Blaine received three red passage tiercels and a very dark and fine passage falcon with the most perfect temper. In the early spring Blaine took these hawks and the two moulted falcons, *Scylla* and *Charybdis*, to the Curragh in Ireland. He was also loaned old *Josephine* by the club and she acquitted herself well, taking twelve rooks in fifteen hawking days. In Blaine's opinion, in most parts the Curragh was too cramped for anything but a double flight. There were, besides, plenty of obstacles in the shape of carts, small parties of cavalry, racing strings, etc., which gave rooks opportunities for foiling the hawks. *Scylla* came on wonderfully well at rooks, going very keen, though stooping too often, but towards the end of the season at Shrewton she much improved, going high and fast and stooping in slashing form.

April 13th. 1906. Blaine's cast flew well and killed. Blaine's horse stampeded, and punctured his hock badly with his spike, I believe. [The spike, attached to a long rein was used to tether the horses while attending to a falcon.] The 'Chasseur's' mustang did likewise, at dusk, and is still ranging the 'grassy prairie', eleven a.m. next day, locality unknown. To have a hawk out is not unknown, but to lose a horse establishes a new record!

Horses certainly created occasional difficulties or near-disasters. The previous season, Clare Garnett, galloping after a flight, took a bad toss. Her mare crossed its feet apparently, turned a complete somersault and was killed instantly, breaking her neck. The gallant rider damaged her leg but had a fortunate escape. On another occasion, while the members were at lunch enjoying a picnic on the plain, all the horses suddenly galloped off when a racing string cantered by, and a lot of valuable hawking time was wasted in recovering them.

In September 1906, the club hawks went to Avebury, hawking partridges on land rented by Mr Garnett. The house next to the Red Lion [later to become a Mecca for falconers] was taken as a shooting lodge, and with three efficient tiercels, and George Oxer and Bob Slightam as falconers, they enjoyed some good sport before hawks and falconers journeyed to Aintree on Lord Sefton's estate for partridge and seagull hawking. *Aimwell* was moulted by Garnett, and had changed every feather by September, particularly early for a passage falcon. She again flew well at Shrewton in the spring of 1907 and helped to make all the young ones, being flown in a cast with them all in turn, and was never at fault when wanted. She was credited with thirty-six rooks and was given her freedom in that summer. *Clairette* proved the best of the young entry with a score of sixty-three rooks.

The rook hawking of 1908 proved one of the worst seasons on record. Rooks were scarce, and heavy snowstorms at Easter made sport impossible. However, the partridge hawking at Avebury was a great success, despite the villainous weather, and two good falcons, *Mary Ann* and *Glory Ann*, were trained by Oxer. Gilbert Blaine, after a season or two at grouse, with little success, had taken Mr Stephen's shooting at Compton in Berkshire – about two thousand acres. Here he was to start producing the successes at game hawking that soon became expected of him. In 1907 Richard Best, Blaine's falconer, had entered two eyases, from the isle of Lundy – a falcon, *Olive*, and a tiercel, *Lundy III* – to partridges, Blaine being away on duty most of the season. The tiercel in particular turned out to be a game hawk of the highest possible class, and in the summer of 1908 Blaine received another three tiercels from the same famous eyrie. They were hacked for five weeks. For the first time Gilbert Blaine also hacked some merlins, keeping three for himself. On 28 September Mr and Mrs Garnett drove over to Compton and spent two enjoyable days with Blaine and his hawks. Mr Garnett noted:

138

Partridge hawking.

'After a successful flight.' Black Lady *on the ground with a
dead partridge.*

Sept. 28th.   The merlins: *Psyche* flew a ringer in style and put in but did not kill. A fine rattling flight. She then, after a refusal or two, hunted one very determinedly and ran into him in deep cover. *Cupid* flew a rattling ringer, and put in same place as *Psyche* but was served and killed.
The peregrines: *Lundy III*, who mounts and waits on magnificently, trussed his first and hit and then caught an old Frenchman, his second flight in the very finest form. *Black Cloud* caught, but let go his first. His second he caught finely in the open. A high flyer and pretty steady. *Olive*, a fairly good second year falcon, caught hers easily, not a high flyer as I saw her. *Lundy IV* flew well and high, rather 'larky', but exceptionally fast, killed his easily.
Sept. 29th.   *Celeste* sat on a bad lark. *Cupid* did the same with a moderate one. We then had the lark flight of my life. *Cupid* and *Psyche* refused a lark but suddenly took on a ringer in lovely country. *Psyche* took six rings to fetch him and was then two rings to the good on the jack. She put in two stoops before he got to work and they then went at him hammer and tongs for two minutes; I never saw such stooping. *Psyche* finally caught him a mile or more downwind. I could just see her with my glasses. We found her with some difficulty in open grass. It was a flight worth crossing England to see. A full moulted lark, adult. A most delightful two days. I have not seen merlins flown for sixteen years. Blaine's were well-mannered, and flew far above any I have ever seen. They refuse, as is to be expected so late in the season, at times, but when they go, they do not mince matters. The sport was of the highest class. His peregrines are good, all of them, but *Lundy III* stands out as a notable hawk, flying high and waiting in reach [over the falconers and dog]. The best peregrines I have seen to date. His tiercels can all fly. His falcon not so good as either of ours.

The three merlins finished up with a score of one hundred and seventy-eight larks, killing their last on 3 October. On the 14th of the month the merlins, fit and well fed, were turned loose. Three days later the little jack merlin, *Cupid*, came in to *Lundy III* as he was sitting on a partridge he had just caught, and proceeded to discuss it with him. The tiercel never touched him. By November the jack had found his way to the hawk lawn in the village and for some time came most mornings to be fed. The peregrines took two hundred and seventy partridges that season.
'A poor season, not enough work for the hawks; never saw so much wind.' So Mr Garnett summed up the rook hawking in 1909. Few members were able to get down at the beginning of the season – only David Scott and Gerald Lascelles – so they were short-handed. Heywood Jones was laid up with a broken leg from a hunting accident, and Blaine was in German East Africa, on safari. The partridge hawking at Avebury went well, with four falcons on the

140

Erin, *a fine eyas falcon*.

'Jack' taking up Mrs Gibson.

cadge. Of the two second-season falcons, *Victress*, née *Olive*, given to
the club by Gilbert Blaine, was unfortunately lost at the end of the
season.

Blaine moved his operations from Berkshire to Wiltshire in the
autumn of 1909 and again started the season with some excellent lark
hawking. He found the country around Larkhill and The Bustard
ideal and once more enjoyed a successful few weeks before the start of
the partridge hawking on 1 September. The weather, on the whole,
was perfect and many high ringing flights occurred.

Friday Aug. 27th.   *Violet* caught three bad larks, and then a ringer got up,
and after a few preliminary turns mounted right into the sky. The merlin
started ringing wide, when a wild hobby came in above her, but could not
fetch the lark. Both hawks and lark continued to go up until the lark was
lost in the blue. The merlin got up too and passed the Hobby, and all three
crossed over a fir plantation downwind. At last, after repeated rings high in
the sky, the merlin fetched the lark and rattled him down past the Hobby
below, where the latter joined in, and each stooping alternately the merlin
footed the lark high in the air, the Hobby binding to it soon afterwards, and
passed out of our sight below the brow of the plain. On approaching I saw
the Hobby making off, and found *Violet* plucking the lark at the corner of a
small plantation. A really fine ringing flight showing great pluck and
determination on the part of the Merlin, who was of course fed up at once.

142

Best with the cadge.

In September, Blaine was invited to join Charles Garnett for the day at Avebury and, although not quite agreeing in their diary comments, nevertheless both parties greatly enjoyed their day. Blaine:

Found plenty of partridges. The Club hawks were not in very good form. Old *Olive* (*Victress*), after putting in a partridge, went off and was lost. The best of their two young falcons, *Maud Allan*, was quite off colour and would not fly. Her sister *Salome* flew well and killed a brace-and-a-half.
Lundy V went magnificently and killed a brace, but was a little too keen. *Old Lundy*, after putting in a single partridge near a sheep fold in one grand stoop, was distracted by pigeons in the village, then went on the soar downwind, and was lost till after lunch, when he turned up when another hawk was being flown. In the evening he killed a brace-and-a-half. *Lundy IV* killed a brace in fine style and George Oxer liked him the best of the three tiercels. E. B. Michell, and several of Garnett's friends out.

Garnett:

Plenty of birds. Blaine brought over three slashing tiercels. *Lundy V* went into the clouds, and fooled after larks, but finally killed his bird well. Again, later he put in, went up and killed when served. *Salome* killed three successively, flying well and fast, but not high. *Lundy IV* killed his first

143

magnificently, from a tremendous height, and flown again did equally as well. I thought him the highest of the lot. *Lundy III*, at his first, put in one grand stoop, but was put out by hurdles. He put in, would not wait, and did not return until 4 p.m. Later on he killed his first brilliantly, his second he took and held actually in turnips. The dogs put him off: he went up and killed another.

Maud Allan killed one in fair style.

So ended the finest days game hawking I have yet seen. Blaine's tiercels were all so good it was hard to choose. The old one (*Lundy III*) stooped rather the best, but is very unsteady, particularly if he sees a pigeon, but the whole performance was of the highest class.

It is always a pleasure for a falconer to see other hawks flown and, indeed, to show off his own hawks, if they are good enough. Both Blaine and Garnett had enjoyed their joint days, both at Avebury and Tilshead, and in September 1910 they again met at Avebury and there achieved a 'record' day.

Sept. 23rd.   Wind N.W. A beautiful hawking day, and a red letter day for Avebury. As far as Blaine and I are concerned, a record bag. Blaine came over from Shrewton with two hawks, and we started on Parson's Farm, Monkton, but could not get birds at first. We drove a nice bit in from over Windmill road and the the fun began. *Evelyn* cut one over very nicely in roots and sat on it. Her second essay, she caught, went head over heels, and he got into the Windmill Road, but caught another when served. Before lunch she cut over a wide one and caught him. After lunch she flew a beautiful uphill flight over the down, and held him. Very good indeed. Two brace.

Lundy IV at a very perfect chance, a skied bird into the wind, from a faultless pitch overhead, took him in fifteen yards, and you could hear the blow. Again near same place, from an equally good pitch, he ran into his bird. Once more he killed one downwind, and closed his performance by killing our sixteenth bird handsomely at 5.15 p.m. *Lemburg* put in, and being served killed from a great pitch. Later he took on a bird we did not see and carried over a broken fence, from a good pitch. His next beat him to cover, and later he footed another one very well, same place. *Puck* was beaten honestly to the penning, but took on a downwind one and scored by the beech planting. Later took another. *Gnome*, Blaine's passage tiercel, unluckily saw a runner, and came down from a good pitch, others got up and he scored. Later, rather wide, he was beaten to cover, but coming back over was served, cut over and caught, a beauty. Finally he had one from low gorse, made a grand stoop and he caught. Blaine's hawks as good as ever. So ended a most perfect day. 16 partridges; 17 flights.

Black Jack *and* Lucifer, *two of Blaine's tiercels, in the van with* Drake, Dido, *and* Boss, *1899.*

The rook-hawking season was yet another bad one, with the wind worse than ever, but one falcon, *Kurregunda* did put in a few fine performances:

May 1st.   The outstanding feature of the day was a flight by *Kurregunda*, above the beehives. She was flown at a rook in a tight place, but though she put in two rattling stoops he refused to put in as he could have done easily, and started ringing. She took him on promptly, and fetched him after five or six rings. Possibly they might have been bolder and wider. He then tried to put in, having drifted over covert, but she put in two stoops as he was falling straight into covert, and caught him about two hundred feet up over trees, second stoop. A very brilliant flight. The result was pretty near perfect.

In September 1912, after the usual partridge hawking on Mr Garnett's manor at Avebury, the club hawks travelled to Aintree with George Oxer, as usual, and had a successful season, taking twenty-nine gulls and fifty-nine partridges there. Bob Slightam, now employed by Lord Howard de Walden, had joined Oxer at Avebury to enter his Lordship's hawks before returning to Cambridgeshire for further partridge hawking.

Once again the rook hawking was not a great success in 1913, but as usual many guests came out to see the sport. One such visitor wrote later that year:

It was about twelve o'clock, when, mounted on my shaggy steed, and accompanied by four or five other falconers, I left the old-world village of Shrewton and set out across the Plain in the direction of Stonehenge. After a short but pleasant canter across the Plain we came up with the Hawking van, in which the hawks were carried on specially constructed perches. Some rooks were soon sighted in a convenient position, well away from any wood or cover into which they might put. . . . When within some three hundred yards or so of the rooks, and while we remain where we are, Oxer proceeds on foot, carrying the hooded falcon on his left fist, a man walking directly in front of him with the idea of screening the peregrine from the 'canny' rooks. Soon the falcon is unhooded and 'thrown off' upwind. The rooks scatter in every direction, but one of them is unfortunate enough to be picked out as a possible victim by the peregrine. A moment later I was riding as fast as my horse's legs would take him with my eyes glued skywards, quite oblivious of rabbit holes or other similar dangers which might be awaiting me. There was now a check, the peregrine mounting fast, and when well over the rook she made as magnificent a stoop as ever I expect to see; but the wily old rook dodged and the peregrine missed her aim. Again she mounted, and the rook was killed outright with 'one fell swoop' within five yards of my horse.

1914 brought better sport, with a useful team of hawks. *Rosalind* looked like making a class hawk, with a fine temper. Rooks were scary and hard to get near. Yet another visitor left some notes of what he saw:

April 15th, 1914.   I went to Shrewton, and put up at the Catherine Wheel. Fine and warm, fresh N.E. breeze. Out on Flower's land via Stonehenge to Durrington Valley . . . *Rosalind* put a flock into a fold, declined to hunt, and went off upwind, putting more rooks into another fold. She then started ringing up after two very high rooks which looked impossible on account of covert all round. However she fetched them in a marvellously short time, killing first stoop still some way short of the covert they had been making for. An extraordinary feat! *Cleone* killed two rooks after short hustles around an old sheep fold. *Delphine* fetched a rook into a young plantation, but when the rook was hustled out, and at her mercy, she would have nothing more to do with him. Flown again, she did not see the rook she was slipped at, took on another upwind, had a couple of stoops and then chucked it and went off upwind over Durrington; luckily she came back to us, but it wasted half an hour.

April 18th.   Bright and hot. Durrington valley all day. *Rosalind* killed two

George Oxer in the garden at Church House, 1914.

Club falcon Rosalind, *1914.*

easy rooks. *Cleone* also killed a sitter, but then got beaten by a real warrior of a rook. *Timandra* (with *Sister B* who refused) fetched rooks well and killed in good style third stoop.

Delphine had a slip of not more than thirty yards at three very confident rooks. She declined! The rooks flopped up, looked at her, and then settled not ten yards further on and began to feed again! This was too much; they were ridden up with yells of rage, which so excited *Delphine* that she came in and caught one. *Sister B* was beaten by a good rook into Larkhill Camp, going in very good form. But once she had put him in, she went straight off upwind to Durrington and was lost. Recovered by Ben Bessent, off a stack in the valley same evening. At the end of the day Oxer was just putting up the haggard falcon, *Melesandre*, to the lure, when a rook came up. The haggard went off after him and fetched him; but George Oxer called her down to a pigeon for no members of the Club were still out.

The Great War. Oxer flew the hawks as usual in the spring of 1915 but then the hawks were dispersed. One, a fine passager, went to Blaine's falconer, Richard Best, who took the grouse hawks to Caithness on his own that autumn. Four other falcons went to London Zoo.

148

9

THE REVIVAL

The Club has been in abeyance during the War, but we hope to revive it. For a first attempt we have done well. Sixty-five rooks to date, and bad weather all April. B. Heywood Jones died just over a year ago, in 1918. It is not for me to write his obituary, but he was a great falconer, a good sportsman all round, and universally liked by all who knew him. Gerald Lascelles has broken down in health and will be with us no more on the Plain, I fear.

The Old Club as we knew it is dead. May a new one arise. I shall miss the genial company of these two at the Church House more than I yet realise.

These words from Charles Garnett's papers were to herald a new beginning of the annals of the Old Hawking Club.

A beginning was made in the spring of 1920, with four passage hawks trapped the previous autumn by Karl Mollen at Valkenswaard. Gilbert Blaine had taken over the management of the club, with headquarters still at Church House in Shrewton.

Blaine had started keeping hawks in 1898, encouraged by Major Charles Hawkins Fisher and Major Eustace Radclyffe. His early successes at partridge on the heathland of Dorset were in part due to the knowledge and skill of Major Fisher's falconer, James Rutford, who acted as falconer to Blaine for his first three partridge seasons, aided by Richard Best. Best started as a young game-keeper to Major Radclyffe, at Hyde in Dorset, and there trained as a falconer under Tom Allen before being employed by Gilbert Blaine, in whose service he remained for twenty-five years. On leaving Dorset at the end of the 1901 season, Blaine had only moderate success until 1907, when he took the partridge manor at Compton in Berkshire. There, as we have already seen, Best trained an outstanding tiercel, *Lundy III*, and, although Blaine was away for much of the season, the hawks put together an excellent score. It was during this season, on 21 October, that Best with Blaine's hawks and spaniel, Boss, met up with George Oxer in London and went down to Audley End to fly their hawks for the benefit of Lord Howard de Walden. So was another enthusiast gathered to the fold. The hawks killed seven brace of partridges, one pheasant, one kestrel and ten rabbits with *Mrs Gibson*, Blaine's goshawk, in four hawking days. Best returned to Berkshire on 2 November to report that the hawks had worked perfectly, but were hampered by the thickness of the root crops and hedgerows, never getting a bird that was cut down or put in. All the kills scored were footed at the first stoop. The goshawk had been flown on only two occasions, catching five rabbits each time, having to stop flying when her wings and tail became too wet from the long grass.

After increasingly successful campaigns at partridges in Berkshire and Wiltshire, Blaine again turned his attention to the grouse moors of Scotland, and in 1912 he took a lease on the Castle of Mey moors in Caithness. His first season was a great success, 1912 being a great grouse year, but there is no doubt that much of that success was due to the excellence of the dogs so ably handled by 'Jack' Frost.

Jack Frost, second son of the famous John Frost, falconer to the Old Hawking Club, had for a time assisted George Oxer with the Club hawks. He had then been employed by Daisy, Countess of Warwick, as falconer, which only lasted a short while. Jack and his newly-wed wife, Kate, took a public house, The Ship, at Lymington, but this did not work out well and before long Jack was back in the falconry business, the family living at Lyddington Warren, about six miles from Swindon in Wiltshire. As a freelance falconer, Jack Frost was engaged for some interesting posts, one being with Prince Sturdza of Rumania. In 1910, Richard Best spent a year in Hungary and Jack Frost was taken on by Blaine for the partridge season as falconer and dog handler, with young Ted Woods to assist him. By this time the Frost family had moved to Shalbourne, renting a large old house with outbuildings called Hillview, where Frost kept his own hawks and dogs. He often set out early to walk across the plain by 10 a.m. in time to attend Blaine's party for a days hawking. For ten days in the middle of the season Frost took his own hawks and a good pointer dog, Nimrod,[1] to France to fulfil a promised engagement, but returned to enjoy what was to be a record year for Blaine's hawks. On Best's return from Hungary, Jack Frost remained a further two seasons with Gilbert Blaine as dog handler; then, buying Noad's House in Tilshead on the plain, he set up as a freelance dog handler,

---

1 Nimrod, a liver-and-white pointer dog, was sold in France for £60.

150

'Jack' Frost, second son of John.

The creators of a successful day . . .

On point.

training Field Trial English setters for three or four gentlemen.

The grouse-hawking season of 1913 was to be a record year for Blaine, with a bag of four hundred and six grouse in fifty-one flying days, probably a record for all time. Once again the setters were responsible for much of the success, and were handled by 'Tommy' Morris. Charles Garnett spent four days at Barrogill Lodge at Mey towards the end of August, and enjoyed all of the incidents:

Aug. 27th. Opened my season with Blaine at Barrogill. A good team, but the old falcons not yet in form. Tiercels going A1.

Aug. 28th. A beautiful day, on the warm side. Shot over dogs till lunch, three brace, and also hawked a brace before lunch. Then the fun began. Dogs worked brilliantly, particularly 'Glee', and we killed four out of one covey in succession, two out of another, and had finished by 5 p.m. Hawks went high and well, Lundy falcon [*Sylvia*] particularly waiting on high upwind. They footed most of them and the tiercels footed three and cut over another dead, with a broken back. The tiercels were very brilliant, and *Gnome* had to kill three to make the (day) record. Thirteen grouse. Best very pleased. I imagine it was grouse hawking of the top notch. Hawks always on the verge of soaring, but never doing so, except *Gnome*, who came up very small and killed from the clouds. 'Glee' is a brilliant ranger, good nose, very steady, and will flush one bird then drop like a stone. Then flush one more, and so on. Honours divided between dogs and hawks. I was hawking alone, as Blaine was shooting with a neighbour.

Aug. 30th. *Barbara* fast improving, both old falcons waiting well upwind. Tiercels as good as ever. The Lundy falcon caught a fowl, fearful ructions from the lady owner. Hawk caught by a crofter who refused to part with her. All ended without hurt. Rather amusing really, but Blaine could not see it. Perhaps excusably. Crum Ewings and party out from Castlehill.

So ends my debut at grouse hawking. Blaine has brought it to a very high pitch of excellence. Good hawks, good management and dogs of the highest class. Three of the dogs I consider better than his winning brace at Lanark last year, and not a bad one in the lot. 'Glee' easily takes the palm for hawking, and I like him best all round.

The tiercels are remarkably good at the game, and keen, particularly the old one (*Lundy III*), who usually had his bird over in fifty yards, and flew very high. *Barbara*, in my opinion, will be best, when she is in full swing.

All of Blaine's old hawks died in the moulting loft at Shrewton during the war. *Barbara*'s death was caused through her being unable to lay a second egg, she having already laid one perfect one. Richard Best lived at Pampas Cottage and from there looked after Blaine's hawks and his dogs, in kennels opposite the Plume of Feathers in Shrewton. Gilbert Blaine spent the war doing good service as an officer in the

Best unhooding Lady Jane.

Best lifting Lady Jane *from a rook kill.*

ammunition columns. Charles Garnett, through ill health, could not join up, but did service with the British Red Cross, using his old car as an ambulance.

Best stooping a falcon at the lure.   *Best throwing off a rook hawk.*

So once again the Old Hawking Club was rook hawking on the plain, and after the small start made in 1920, with only four hawks, three of which turned out well, more hawks were ordered from Mollen. Four passage falcon and two haggards arrived in November, enabling Best, who had taken over the post of head falconer to the club, to start the 1921 season with a team of nine falcons.

A new member of the club, Captain K. R. Palmer, travelled down to Church House for the first time on 23 March. He had sent down Comet and Serviette, two of his polo ponies, the day before and going out for the first time with hawks on the 24th was fascinated by it all. It was a fine sunny day, with practically no wind. Blaine and the Allens were out (Major Stanley Allen was another of the pre-war brigade). Seven flights – four kills.

March 25th.   . . . The eagle owl was used today for the first time, and with great success – the rooks coming in well to mob him in the open, thus affording Best some good slips. . . . I managed to get one more day's Rook Hawking on the 3rd. May when I motored down for the day. Six flights and five kills. *Dawn* flew two excellent flights, and *Titania* an exceptionally good one. Blaine and the Garnetts out.

Charles Garnett was out with the hawks as often as possible, motoring over from Chippenham with his wife and children. Kit, his son, later became a member of the club.

154

Palmer with Christmas, *1921*.

The eagle owl belonging to the Old Hawking Club.

April 6th.   Today was an ideal day, if a little warm. The plain is in its best 'iron' condition. Blaine has done well, killing forty rooks to date. We should have gone to pieces without him. Captain Palmer, a new recruit, has been out a few weeks, but had to stop and return to barracks owing to the coal strike. Stanley Allen also up for a time, but now gone. Also Portal. We hawked from the car, Blaine the only cavalry man. *Dawn*, a beautiful haggard, and very tractable, killed her first rook, first stoop in the Classical style. Again, at a crow, beyond Tilshead valley, was beaten upwind at last, after a good flight. Flown again, put into a tree, could not be served and finally chucked it after a long hunt. Went on the soar and taken down by Gilbert Blaine. Very unlucky, but a class hawk.

April 13th.   *Mary Rose*, near Elbarrow, killed second stoop on a side wind. Later she changed to a pigeon passing under her, when she had her rook beaten and was lost. *Dawn* killed her first rook in classic style, first stoop, out of a flock. Later, same place, she flew a fine flight at a ringing bunch, and killed. *Titania*, same place, killed third stoop, very deadly, but might go higher and do better.

April 28th.   Rather a large field out of a mixed nature. Lord Lansdowne and Lord Kerry in a Ford car. Clare, Kit and Barbara. *Sport and General* photographer and a cinema man! *Dawn* our first flight, most lucky. Right over Lord L. in the car, half a dozen good stoops and a kill after a long hunt in a fold. A good class flight, and very showy. She killed twice more, as we were short of hawks. *Mary Rose* killed two well and honestly today. *Lady Jane* killed her first, a high grand flight, which we missed through coffee-housing and gossiping. Her second she got a good rook and put him into a fold, but would not stoop over the sheep and finally went off and killed upwind in the Tilshead road. Luckily picked her up in a rainstorm. A successful day to a whole field of spectators. One really nice exhibition flight.

The rook hawks for the season were:

Titania, first-season passage falcon. LOST. This was a tragedy as she was a fine flyer, though rather a bad temper.
Mary Rose, first-season passage falcon. She started the season well, flying in fine style, but she was an unlucky falcon and towards the end of the season began to fly cunning. Being moulted by Garnett.
Quanza, first-season passage falcon. LOST. She was a good flyer but bad at catching rooks.
Dawn, haggard falcon. By far the best rook hawk of the year, and probably one of the finest the Club has ever had.
Lady Jane, second-season passage falcon. A fine rook hawk on her day.
Whitewings, a second-season passage falcon. A very beautiful and large falcon with great character. She did not like rooks and would rarely fly them.

156

White Wings, *1922*.   *Ken Palmer with* White Wings.

Mary Rose, *the passage falcon belonging to the Club, 1921.*

On the grouse moor. Partners Blaine and Palmer in front of the cadge.

Camster Lodge. The temporary building between the lodge and outbuildings were put up to house Blaine's extensive staff.

(The above hawks belonged to G. Blaine.)
Destiny, a second-season passage falcon. LOST. A good hawk and very tame.
Ishanthe, a very old haggard. Useless.
(The above two hawks belonged to S. Allen:)
Falconers: R. Best (employed by Blaine)
          E. Woods (employed by Palmer)
          G. Blake (employed by Blaine)

On 5 August Gilbert Blaine and Ken Palmer arrived at Camster
Lodge, a small grey house surrounded by lovely moorland, but somewhat more hilly than that at Mey. In fact the lodge was not big
enough to house the whole entourage and Blaine had built an annexe
to the main house to house staff. The previous season, Gilbert Blaine
had enjoyed a quiet but successful season with two of the passage
falcons, *Whitewings* and *Lady Jane*, which had been used for rooks
that first season at Shrewton after the war. Joining forces with Blaine,
Palmer rented additional land adjoining Camster, and hoping for a
good season he sent the falconers north with eight falcons. The hawks
had journeyed up by sea, and had a very uncomfortable journey, but
all arrived in good health. Two eyases, from different eyries, had
been taken at Portland, one eyas from the Horn Head eyrie (all
hacked for five weeks at Shrewton), and a lovely falcon, *Arethusa*,
came, in exchange for a tiercel, from Stanley Allen. Having enjoyed

Hawks, dogs and 'field' on the road.

success with the passage falcons at grouse the previous year, Blaine had brought up a new passage falcon, *Ruth*, but she proved a complete failure at grouse and was sent south to Charles Portal to try at partridges. At first none of the eyases showed signs of waiting on, so they were entered to gulls. *Dawn*, the haggard, after killing twelve grouse in good style, voluntarily transferred her interest to gulls and proved to be as outstanding at that quarry as she had been at rooks in the spring.

Sat. Sept. 17th.   Wind E. Fine and clear. A perfect hawking day. *Dawn* slipped at three young Herring Gulls at the Shepherd House rubbish dump, took on a good one and after about three stoops caught it, but slipped it again as they were falling. The gull then began to ring with the Falcon after it. She kept over it at first, but rested her wings twice and let it get a start. After getting up fairly high she gave up and turning went hard up the valley to other gulls, and getting over them stooped hard and caught one, but slipped him as she had the first one. The gull then began to ring, and the Falcon also. They went on ringing until they were both an immense height in the air, and drifting downwind towards Kensary all the time. At one time it looked as though she would never get over him, but she persevered, and at last by zigzagging and going out wider, she got on a level with him. She still kept on, and the gull began to falter in his upward flight, and then *Dawn* got right over him and in a short perpendicular stoop trussed him. They began to fall from that immense altitude quite slowly, but when a third of the distance to earth, a wild falcon came in from the north, and hung onto the gull. Both then let go, and the gull fell earthwards with his wings spread, both hawks stooping after him. *Dawn* got hold again a long time before reaching the ground, and all three disappeared over the horizon.

Best marked the line well, and I picked her up nearly two miles from where she had been slipped, on the open flow ground near the lower end of the Bothy Burn. She was unruffled, so the wild hawk had not crabbed her.

The finest flight of any sort I have ever witnessed by a trained hawk, marred only by the incident of the check from one gull to another. The game hawks went spendidly.

Of the eyases, *Christmas* turned out well at seagulls, flown in a cast, and was to perform well at the rooks the following spring. Blaine went over to Valkenswaard to collect the new passage falcons and returned in November with five red falcons and two haggards. Palmer took two of the red falcons - *Miranda*, a strong temperamental hawk with a lovely eye, and *Lavinia*, a very gentle falcon and like a wooden hawk to hood. Stanley Allen took two passagers. One died of the 'croaks', but the other a small falcon, *Princess*, turned out well. Portal's red

160

falcon died of 'croaks', as did Millers's, but the real disaster was the loss of *Dawn*, who escaped through an open window towards the end of February and was not recovered. Unfortunately, she was not belled, and although Best saw her one day at Prospect Farm he had little hope of getting her back. That winter Blaine had managed to cure her of a bad attack of 'frounce' and she was fit and well, but she was greatly missed in the spring of 1922. Garnett noted of her: '*Dawn* was lost from the mews through an open window. An irreparable loss of a very great hawk, and she is badly missed in an otherwise moderate team.'

That spring Blaine received a long telegram from the Allied Cinema Company, asking if he had a 'trained hunting falcon' for disposal as Douglas Fairbanks wanted one for his next film, *Robin Hood*. Blaine wrote to Ken Palmer suggesting that *Minerva*, the Horn Head eyas of the previous year, was just the falcon to suit them, being very tame and easy to handle, and indeed a poor performer at grouse, gulls or rooks. The falcon was offered for £50 (fresh caught passage falcons at that time costing £3. 10*s*. each), which the company accepted! The hawk had to sail immediately on the *Augustania* en route for Los Angeles. The hawk was delivered, personally, and Blaine and Palmer had a most amusing interview with the manager and several others. The officials of the film company were shown how to handle the falcon and a short essay was dictated, and taken down in shorthand, on the basic elements of falconry. The usual idiotic questions were asked by various Americans present, such as 'What do you put the hood on for?', 'I've kept a parrot so I know what to do with this bird!', etc. The manager was very anxious that Palmer should take the falcon to Los Angeles, and offered to pay all expenses and a handsome fee. When he remarked that he would not go to Los Angeles for a fortune, they were astonished. Before leaving, *Minerva* was crated up, and the handler seemed reasonably confident and competent. As Palmer noted: ' . . . I hope she will prove herself a better hawk on the cinema than she was in the field.'

It was not a good rook season in the spring of 1922. Blaine and Stanley Allen were away most of the early part of the season, the weather was cold and windy, and it was difficult to find rooks out in suitable places. On 10 April, Charles and Kit Garnett went over and endured a terrible day:

A shocking day, every hawk lost, practically every flight, though recovered, and we killed two rooks neither of which was flown at! Almost the worst exhibition I have ever seen. I fear they are a poor lot. We lost much time looking for hawks. *Ariadne* was spotted by Kit, but it took us an hour or more to collect our field together again. We were lucky to bring them all home.

April 17th. . . . *Christmas*, at Prospect, flew a real classic flight, killing second stoop. She is an undeniable flyer.

Ken Palmer, who owned this eyas falcon, which was putting up the occasional performance better than that shown by the passage hawks, wrote of the same flight:

Christmas, given a very long and difficult slip at a rook on passage, put up the best performance so far, this season: the rook went up very quickly and the falcon had to go very hard and high into the wind to fetch him, which she did, putting in a smashing stoop which brought him down: she then threw up beautifully and caught him with her second stoop. It was in every way a high class performance. Garnett and party of four out. The previous day horses caused problems. At one moment after lunch, all the horses escaped. Blaine also had problems with his pony. The pigeon escaped from his pocket and got its line entangled round the pony's legs, and Blaine landed up on his back. Both pigeon and pony lost. Pony recovered later!

The hawks improved a little as the season progressed, but continued to be unlucky:

April 20th. *Christmas* was flown four times, but it was not one of her days! She ought to have killed each time if she had not played about with her rooks – the first flight she was slow in fetching, but put in three good stoops, the rook putting into a rick when she chucked it – the last flight she shepherded the rook very well, and put in a terrific stoop, just missing her rook, and she could not recover herself, striking the ground with a resounding thump and was knocked out; however, she recovered after about a minute and came into the lure. *Miranda* fetched rather slowly, but manoeuvred well and killed first stoop: flown again she was most unlucky – the flight ending in a long hunt round a rick when she knocked the rook over about the tenth stoop, and did not recover herself, hitting the ground hard – she was dazed but got on the wing again and came in to the lure. Ted had slipped her earlier with her leash and swivel on! She was at once got down to the lure. *Lavinia* fetched well and killed second stoop. *Princess* went very well, stooping and throwing up in good style, and killing third stoop . . . Practically every day we see a wild peregrine. I hope this means the noble race is increasing. Mr. and Mrs. Scott out.

April 25th. . . . *Miranda* was slipped at two rooks on passage near the Fox covert and a wonderful ringing flight resulted – Best says it was one of the

Camster, 1921. A cast of hawks on a gull.

finest flights he has ever seen. The falcon started slowly and the rooks at once got well above her, however she meant business and made a succession of splendid wide rings; By the time the Tilshead road was reached they were all an immense height, the falcon still ringing after them. When nearly over the trees in Orcheston village, the rooks made a short dive for cover, but realising that they could not get there, they started to ring up again, the falcon still sticking to them. They were still at a great height. A few seconds later they made a dive for the trees at Elston House and *Miranda* put in a long slanting stoop at them – her first – but did not catch; she threw up and caught one of them in her second stoop still high in the air, and they came to earth between Orcheston and Elston House. I should not have believed *Miranda* capable of a flight like this! The Allens out.

Only ninety-eight rooks were taken in the season and three falcons lost in the last week.

At Camster 1922 was to be a record year to equal 1913, with a total of four hundred and six grouse taken by the hawks. The season was the more remarkable in that nearly all of Gilbert Blaine's fine kennel of English setters died of distemper shortly after their arrival in Caithness, leaving just three old dogs and one bitch puppy to do all the work, both shooting and hawking. Only a falconer who hawks grouse can fully understand how serious the loss of dogs is to the chance of a successful season. Ten hawks were taken north but five of them were responsible for nearly the whole score of grouse. Of these five, two – a tiercel and a falcon, brother and sister – produced the highest scores, although the best of the three other falcons, the

163

The grouse hawks at Camster, 1922. Lundy *is in the foreground, with* White Wings *on the left and* Lady Jane *on the right.*

The cadge, at Camster, 1922.

intermewed passage falcon *Lady Jane*, equalled the tiercel's score, though taking longer to do it. The two young eyases had been hacked for six weeks at Shrewton, and it was only by chance that they managed to snare the tiercel as he had been absent from the feeding blocks for three days. A fine young eyas from a Devon eyrie was the only hawk lost in Caithness, going clean out of sight towards Wick after a fine ringing flight at a gull. A great loss, as she was sister to Charles Portal's wonderful partridge falcon *Sibella*. The haggard falcon, *Ariadne*, was a failure at grouse, and would not wait on. Ken Palmer's tiercel, *Lundy*, was the undoubted star of the team, both Blaine and Best considering him the smartest tiercel they had ever seen. He killed seventy-five grouse and one snipe with only five misses. He mounted high from the very beginning, and later in the season went too high, if that be possible. In the middle of the season he became somewhat unsteady and was nearly lost on several occasions. He was a small tiercel with a particularly small foot. As Palmer remarked, 'I hope he may live for another ten seasons!'

The rook season of 1923 was a disaster. Garnett wrote:

The hawks are a sorry lot, all going wrong. Knight lost two at home before the season ever began. Palmer lost his flying first day – too wild. Finally left with four hawks: *Ariadne*, moulted by me and well summered, but now croaking; *Christmas*, now belonging to Allen, a rogue this year; *Diana*

(Langford's falcon) no use and never will be except to crab another hawk; and *Althaea* (Blackall Simmonds), a good falcon.

After such a bad season in the spring of 1923, a great effort was made to do better and more falcons were ordered that autumn from Mollen. Owing to the exceptionally rough weather, only six hawks were caught and all retained by the club. The six consisted of three red falcons, one haggard falcon, and two red tiercels. Fortunately, Dwyer caught a grand passage falcon in his plover nets in Ireland, so these, together with two old hawks, made up the team at Shrewton in March 1924.

Gilbert Blaine had not returned from Abyssinia by 24 March, so Charles Garnett and Palmer opened the season with a most successful day.

March 24th.   Captain Palmer and I opened the season with five passage falcons, one haggard, one gull hawk (eyas) and two passage tiercels. They seem a fairly likely lot. I like the Irish falcon (*Donegal*) as well as any as regards form. She is fast and seems clever.
The owl has been requisitioned again from the Zoo. He should prove a valuable decoy again. Rooks this spring seem near extinct.
Eight double flights at Yarnbury, on one piece of sown land, as fast as we could fly them. Five rooks killed, one right and left, in seven flights. The haggard was lost, on a kill, but I found her. Leonard managed to get near her and wound her up.

Every season is usually remembered by certain incidents or by an outstanding hawk. The season of 1924 might well have been remembered as the year of lost and recovered hawks, although *Donegal* and *Agrippa*, the haggard, were finally lost for good.

April 19th.   The most unlucky day's hawking on record! Lost *Donegal*, although slipped in a perfect place. Hunted for her until 4 p.m. unsuccessfully. We then lunched and decided to have another flight in the same place in the hope that it might bring up *Donegal*. *Agrippa* was given a perfect slip at rooks mobbing the owl – she flew her rook hard but was eventually beaten to the rookery; she would take no notice of lures and went off towards Winterbourne Stoke – we spent until 9 p.m. looking for her without result. As I rode into Shrewton a man stopped me and said he had seen a hawk sitting on the ground near Leslie's Farm – I went back and found her – it was *Bluefoot*!! She hadn't even been taken out hawking. The staple of her block had come away and she had gone off, swivel and leash, about 6 p.m. This was the limit! Two flights, two lost hawks and one lost from the block!!

Bluefoot, *a falcon in her first season.*

20th.   Searched from 5 a.m. till 2 p.m., no success, although *Piga* was found. [She had been lost on the 18th.]

21st.   *Nydia* lost!!

22nd.   Spent the whole day looking for lost hawks. In the evening a man brought in *Donegal* – she flew a woodpigeon into his toolshed near Berwick St. James, and he caught her. The man said that he had heard that they (hawks) bite, so he got a two pronged fork, and pinned *Donegal* down to the ground; he then caught her round the neck! and put her in a tiny wooden box, with a piece of wire netting on top: She seems none the worse for her adventure.

23rd.   We had news of a hawk in Westdown Valley . . . After a long search we found her roosting at the rookery, but she wouldn't come to anything shown her. Best thinks it is *Nydia*.

24th.   Best went out at daybreak, but the hawk went away after rooks. Lost *Donegal*.

25th.   I went out at daybreak and we got *Nydia*. We could find no trace of *Donegal*.

26th.   Garnett returned from the north this morning. He went out with *Piga* in the evening and she killed two rooks in very rough weather. Second flight she caught her rook on a window sill of the farm at the foot of Breech Hill and carried it into the porch. The farmer caught both falcon and rook, but let both go again. The rook departed, but *Piga* went into the parlour and was shut in. Not approving of her surroundings, she flew like a bullet through the window pane, and sat down outside! Apparently none the worse.

29th.   We found *Donegal* about 5 p.m., at Tilshead, where she had killed and eaten a rook. Didn't get her.

166

2nd. May . . . *Piga* refused an easy chance in Westdown Valley, and went off and killed in a water cart – a ploughman shut the lid, caught *Piga*, and put her in a sack!

5th. May . . . *Piga* was given an awkward slip on Chitterne Hill. She tried hard and put the rook in the trees by the village; she then went off towards Breech Hill and caught a rook in the garden of the farm. The owner removed her to the house, and I found her quietly plucking her victim in the parlour. Evidently she likes this farmhouse!

7th. A bad day for the last of the season. *Phoebe* soared downwind and was lost. Best recovered her a week later.

So a moderate season ended with fifty-four rooks caught in twenty-five flying days.

About ten days before the passage hawks were due to arrive from Holland, in November 1924, a fire broke out at the Shrewton premises and they were totally destroyed – the hawk house burning like matchwood. Guy Blaine's two cars were badly damaged, but fortunately there were no hawks there at the time. The club was lucky enough to be able to rent a wooden hut belonging to the Wiltshire County Council Educational Committee as a mews, for a rental of £20 a year. There was enough room for the falcons to be put on blocks to weather indoors. Gilbert Blaine had completely renovated Noad's House in Tilshead, and had made it most comfortable. The ponies were also now stabled in Tilshead, which made a far better hawking centre.

At about the same time as the old Shrewton headquarters were burnt down, Charles Garnett died suddenly. He was the longest-serving member of the club and a loyal supporter, particularly through the troubled times caused by the war. A cheerful enthusiast, he was the most regular of participants during the rook-hawking season, usually accompanied by his equally enthusiastic wife and family. He was an all-round sportsman, hunted with the Beaufort Hounds, and he was an accomplished shot and a naturalist of repute.

Mollen sent over seven passage falcons, two haggards and two red tiercels. Blaine and Palmer kept a tiercel each, the rest going to Best in Tilshead. They were a nice lot and wintered well in the new premises, although one of the haggards was a bad jumper and was not flown at rooks. Gilbert Blaine was there to help in their training and entering and, all the hawks shaping well, there was hope of a good season once again.

Ken Palmer, who stayed with Blaine for much of the season, considered that it turned out a moderate rook season, although

Outside the Black Horse, Tilshead.

certainly an improvement on the previous two:

. . . the Hawks were out thirty-four days and they killed ninety-four rooks. The hawks were certainly above the average and the weather quite good on the whole, but our country still gets worse and worse every year. The increase of barbed wire is very noticeable and is an enormous handicap. This, and the fact that we are barred from a very large tract of the best country by the daily artillery firing, will, I fear, successfully drive us away in the near future. There is a rumour that the Tank Corps is coming from Lulworth to take up its permanent quarters at Imber – if this is true it will mean that a further tract of country will go. [It did.] An increasing number of people are taking an interest in the sport and on several occasions this season we had a large field out. The Old Hawking Club has got three new members – Lord Howard de Walden, who used to be a member before the war; George Blackall-Simmonds; and young Kit Garnett – and two new subscribers – Captain Blew-Jones and Mr. Pye. Our new headquarters at Tilshead were a great success, and it is a much better centre than Shrewton.

Indeed there were some large fields out, but things did not always go well on those occasions:

30th. April   A most disastrous day without one redeeming feature, as usual when there is a large field out. *Hurrybelle*, given a bad passage slip at a

168

Peregrines at hack, Tilshead.

single rook, when others were downwind, did not fetch and turned away for the downwind rooks which easily beat her to the New Copse rookery. Guy and I were quickly on the spot but the falcon vanished in a mysterious way. All hands – excepting the numerous spectators, who no doubt pondered on the delights of rook hunting during their wait of two hours – set forth in search – G.B. went towards Prospect and I on a fake scent which led me nearly at Shrewton whence I was retrieved by Michell's car to learn that Best had at length found the falcon near the Lavington Road. A belated lunch took place – one party of spectators having departed! . . . It was now raining steadily so we went on by cars to the Tilshead Road where eventually *Primrose* was flown, and killed her rook . . . and so ended an appalling day. Among others, Sir George Noble, Simmonds, Mrs. and Miss Garnett, Michell, etc.

No new eyases were hacked for the grouse hawking in the summer of 1925, Blaine and Palmer relying on the old hawks and four of the new hawks that had been sent by Mollen the previous autumn. Ted Woods and George Blake took them north, and arrived on 27 July. It was not a good season. Many of the hawks were first-class, but the weather was appalling. For twelve consecutive days in the middle of the season the hawks could not be flown. The old eyas tiercel, *Lundy*, was as good as ever, but flew his best late in the day - if flown early he was inclined to play the fool. Blaine had found this with other old hawks in previous years. The new entry, in particular the passage tiercel, were a failure at grouse in what was to be Blaine's last season at Camster, a place that would always hold pleasant memories for him and Palmer.

Mollen sent over four passage falcons, one haggard and a tiercel for the 1926 season. Three of the old hawks had moulted well, but only *Primrose* was to prove any good at rooks in her second season. Blaine was out throughout the whole season, with only occasional help from other members of the club. Sport was of the highest quality, until, after losing four hawks in quick succession, - as always, the better hawks in the team - Blaine called an end to operations. Owing to the rapid increase in the use of barbed wire all over the country, Blaine used cars to follow the hawks and did away with the 'cavalry', the horsemen being so much handicapped in their movements by the wire. This made it impossible to follow up a soaring hawk or a long flight.

The loss of two or three of the best hawks in the middle of the season put an abrupt end to what might have turned out a very successful year. Without *Primrose* one could not carry on, having only *Andromeda* left as the one reliable hawk to fly at rooks. So after a week's fruitless search for the missing hawks, the Secretary returned to London. These hawks were all lost in the same way: - After putting a rook in or, in the case of *Primrose*, chucking it after a couple of stoops, they went up on the soar, remaining in sight for some considerable time, and then stooped into distant rooks (seen through Field glasses). Had that been the end of it, no doubt these hawks would have been picked up without further trouble, but in each case on going by car to the place marked by the glasses, the hawks were nowhere to be found, and had evidently gone on again in some other direction, and no mob [of rooks marking the kill] being seen, was not found that day. These hawks were all in very high condition - the conditions of game hawks - and no doubt found it easy to catch a rook whenever they wanted to. They were refusing all lures, and when a rook persistently does that, the next stage is the inevitable losing of her. It is questionable whether being entirely dependent on motor cars as a means of following hawks, one does not run the greater risk of losing them if anything goes wrong. It is very doubtful whether the Old Hawking Club will continue in being. There are too many obstacles in the way of a fair measure of success, as far as concerns rook hawking. Two good young rook hawks were trained this year, namely *Beeswing* and *Andromeda*; the former, a very small neat hawk, flew from the first in a clever and artistic

170

style. She was lost. The latter, a larger and more powerful falcon, began rather clumsily by flying on the tail of the rook after one or two stoops. She was then flown in double flights with the old haggard, *Augusta*, who was always willing to go with another hawk, and after some time her style improved. She was then flown singly and became really good, finishing up by topping the score with twenty-six rooks. *Primrose* was a really good rook hawk this year. Fast, a fine dashing stooper, and she would hunt well. She had never been lost before until the unfortunate day when she disappeared for good over Larkhill Camp. She had always been a most obedient and honest hawk, and her loss was a real misfortune. The hawks were out on twenty-four days and they killed seventy-nine Rooks.

Here endeth. . . .

10
THE END
AND A
BEGINNING

For sixty-two years, the Old Hawking Club and its members had been the backbone of falconry in these islands. Through its good offices many were able to set up their own establishments, often with hawks passed on by the club, and employing falconers that had served their apprenticeship under John Frost or George Oxer. Now it was all over and the Old Hawking Club had ceased to exist.

Fortunately for falconry, there were many who continued to keep their own hawks. Some, like Lord Howard de Walden, had been members of the club, but keeping their own mews and employing their own falconer, and continued to enjoy the sport they loved so well. Lord Howard de Walden, with his falconer, Brad, who had succeeded Slightam, continued to fly eyas peregrines at partridges near Newmarket, and Major Stanley Allen still rented partridge ground near Tilshead. Palmer went up to Caithness as usual in 1926 for some grouse hawking, but as he remarked in his diary:

Altogether a lot of changes have taken place since the last grouse hawking season. The Old Hawking Club has ceased to exist, and I have parted with Ted Woods. Best is coming up to me for the season as falconer, fishing ghillie and what not! and afterwards his future is undecided. When Ted left me in July I sent *Lundy* and *Lady Jane* down to Best.

It was a disastrous season. Old *Lady Jane* died before she got to Caithness and *Lundy*, after killing four grouse and a snipe, became partially paralysed and had to be destroyed: 'Thus ended the life of probably the best Tiercel that has ever flown in the annals of Falconry.' Richard Best went to live at The Villa, Hawley House, in Hampshire, working for Ken Palmer's father.

During the past few years, it had become the custom for a 'Falconers' Feast' to be held in London each November, on or near St

Michell out lark hawking
near Shrewton.

Michell lifting a merlin from
a corn stook.

Martin's Day. There falconers would meet by invitation to enjoy an excellent meal, good wine and entertaining stories.

On St. Martin's Day 1925, the annual 'Falconers' Feast' was given by Mr. E. B. Michell at the Junior Oxford and Cambridge Club in Stratton Street, and among the guests were, Mr. Gilbert Blaine, Mr. Robert Awdry, Sir Theodore Cook, Mr. Charles Knight, Mr. Hugh Knight, Mr. Sam Sprigg, and Mr. G. Blackall-Simonds. The solid portion of the feast was exclusively composed of game of various kinds, and the subsequent discussion was conducted on a foundation of burgundy and port which proved entirely satisfactory.

E. B. Michell, the most prolific contributor of articles and reports on hawking to various sporting papers, was as early as the late 1870s enjoying conspicuous success with merlins, lark hawking on the Wiltshire Downs. He often joined forces with Colonel Sandford and his merlins, and later with Mr Gardner, which added some friendly competition to the proceedings. Certainly, Michell enjoyed competition. At one time he was referred to as the most outstanding oarsman of all time, with a record as winner of the Diamond Skulls; he was a boxer of renown, starting his career before the use of gloves, and was a champion at light, middle and heavy weights. He was a scholar in classics at Cambridge, a barrister, and when confined to Paris during the seige in the Franco-Prussian war of 1870 he con-

173

sidered rats a luxury! He wrote not only on falconry but also as an expert on curries and on boxing, and he codified the laws of Siam. Many young falconers were helped and encouraged by Michell, and his book *The Art and Practice of Hawking*, published at the turn of the century, started many a budding falconer in quest of hawks and falconers.

Stanley Allen was only in his second term at Harrow when he trained his first sparrowhawk, and was befriended by Michell, who presented him with a copy of his newly published book. In his autobiographical notes Stanley Allen tells a story of Michell's willingness to use his fists:

On his way by train from his home at Bruton to Shrewton with two merlins he wished to fly there, two drunk men entered the carriage and sat opposite the merlins which had been placed unhooded on the seat. After a time one of the men opened his drunken eyes and, astonished at what he saw, pointed his finger unsteadily close to the birds, upsetting them, at the same time trying to arouse his companion to see them. Mr. Michell warned him to stop, but as he did not do so, gave him a straight left, from which he fell back half knocked out. When he came round, thinking his mate had done it, he dropped him one. At the next station both were at it hammer and tongs on the floor when the guard was called and the contest continued on the platform.

Both Stanley Allen and his wife Audrey were such enthusiasts of falconry that they named one of their daughters Merlin and one Kestrel, and, as Stanley said, would have named their son Peregrine, but was put off by the memory of a very pale-faced boy at school who rejoiced in that name and was nicknamed 'Pea Green'.

For some time Stanley Allen lived in London, but kept peregrines and at weekends would go down to Wiltshire to join his falconer to fly them on the plain. A falconer's mind has room for only one thing and all else is forgotten, and so it happened when on one occasion Stanley went down to Wiltshire alone, leaving his wife in charge of family and home. He had received demands for rates, which he had forgotten all about, and on his return home, full of enthusiasm for the sport he had enjoyed, he was shaken to see tickets for sale attached to all his furniture and carpets. Shortly after his departure for Wiltshire a bailiff had arrived and ticketed everything. Fortunately Mrs Allen had some money and the nanny had her savings, they paid the overdue rates. But they had left the tickets everywhere to shock Stanley on his return – which indeed it did.

Both before and after the First World War, Stanley Allen flew rooks in the spring with the Old Hawking Club and hawked partridges in the autumn about Tilshead and Shrewton. It was in 1913 that he was visited for the first time by Charles Portal, then an Oxford undergraduate, who had first been introduced to falconry in 1907 when he was invited by Gilbert Blaine to see partridge and lark hawking in Berkshire. He had not been out rook hawking before and Stanley explained how difficult a quarry the rook could be, and how cleverly a rook could evade the stoop of a falcon. The first flight and the rook was killed instantly. The young Charles Portal must have thought it very easy until they discovered that the rook was blind in one eye. Other flights lived up to expectations. In 1915 Stanley Allen was sent as Ordnance Officer to the Third Cavalry Division – though often the cavalry could not be used for barbed wire stopped war horses as effectively as it did those of the falconers on Salisbury Plain. The cavalry was continually being moved up to where a breakthrough might be made, and suffered heavy casualties, as they could not take cover in the same way as the infantry. Eventually the Germans advanced almost to Amiens and were attacked there. The Canadian cavalry divisions who were to take part followed up the tanks and machine-gun teams. That morning there were thirty-four thousand mounted men in the Boves valley. As Allen remarked in his memoirs, it was a sight never to be forgotten by all who were there.

After the war Stanley Allen, now living at Denne Hill, the family home near Canterbury, once again returned to his hawking, hunting and shooting and in the early 1920s he and Charles Portal (later to become Marshal of the Air Force the Viscount Portal of Hungerford) enjoyed outstanding success at partridges, renting some three thousand acres of first-class ground at one shilling an acre rent.

In November 1927 George Blackall-Simonds invited a number of friends to a 'Falconers' Feast', and at this dinner those present decided to form a new club. The confraternity present included Sir Theodore Cook, editor of *The Field*, Stanley Allen, Sir James Kingston Fowler, Phillott, Langford, Newall, Charlton Anne, Sir George Noble, Gilbert Blaine, Charles Portal and Hugh Knight. This new club was to be known as The British Falconers' Club. Mr Blackall-Simonds was elected as first President and Sir Theodore Cook as Hon. Secretary.

The following year the British Falconers' Club held a meeting on 13 November. At that meeting, Richard Best, Blaine's old falconer, was elected as professional falconer to the club, but unfortunately he died on 1 March 1929. At that same meeting Hugh Knight was

Stanley Allen with Basil Chamberlain.

Norman Knight with a female sparrowhawk.

elected as Hon. Secretary, owing to the death of Sir Theodore Cook.

The Knight family were others who had been helped and encouraged by Michell, and as early as 1913 Charles Knight had been writing to James Harting for advice about sparrowhawks. Not all falconers were as encouraging as Michell or Harting, but most would be helpful to beginners except in time of war:

Dear Captain Knight, – I am always very glad to help anyone in hawking matters but I am afraid nothing at all is going on at present. Our Club is shut down during the war; our falconer is doing other work, and most of our members are on active service of one kind or another. I am afraid there is nothing to do but to wait for happier times when I hope our old sports may revive and go on, as nearly as may be as in former days.

You ask of peregrines. Haggards are no use except in the hands of very experienced falconers and that when they have been properly caught at the right time of year. You should begin with eyases, a good old falcon or tiercel well trained to partridges is what you want, you might learn from her. I know of no such thing to be had at present.

If you will get the Badminton Library volume on Coursing and Falconry, you will find, if you read it carefully, pretty well all I can tell you about hawking and save yourself asking questions.

Dwyer could probably catch a passage peregrine for you in October or November in his plover nets, but I hope you will not be offended if I tell you straight out that you will no more train it and fly it than buy a fiddle and

play a concerto on it if you have never tried before. And I doubt if Gibbs
would do much better.
Yours sincerely,
Gerald Lascelles

Other falconers suggested where hawks might be obtained, if not
already promised to others.

Dear Capt. Knight, – Yours of 23rd. inst. has followed me here – I return
home tomorrow – Not having heard from you I promised to let Mr. Michell
have any nests of merlins my friend in S. Wales could take, so please write or
see him. I cannot do more as I am quite an invalid.

I never had a merlin that wouldn't take a lark in fair flight, and one of my
merlins took twelve larks in an afternoon. Many of the flights being ringers.
If your merlin won't stick to her quarry there must be something wrong with
the trainer or the lark, and it wouldn't be the lark! The sooner you write to
Michell the better – Hoping you will have a successful campaign.
Yours faithfully
Robert Gardner
P.S. I liked the photograph of your kestrel in *Country Life.*

Soon Hugh Knight was organising a gathering of falconers for lark
hawking at Avebury in Wiltshire, and by 1929 this was well
established, with a large tract of land at their disposal, due to
Knight's quiet, persuasive powers. A cheerful group assembled in
August, as Ken Palmer reported in his diary:

I heard from Hugh Knight that he was making up a party to go down to the
'Red Lion' at Avebury for three weeks' lark hawking, and he kindly asked
me to join them, and thus see some lark hawking for the first time, which I
had very much wanted to do for some years, but could never achieve it as I
was always in Caithness in August. I arrived at the Red Lion on the 19th.
August and found a very cheery party assembled, consisting of – among
others – Hugh Knight and Mrs. Knight, Norman Knight, Chas. Knight,
Blackall-Simonds, Stanley Allen, Read, Hendley and two American friends
of Chas's. The Inn was of the old-fashioned variety, very comfortable and
good plain food, landlord, William James Stagg. We had some excellent
sport and, as I always thought I should be, I was very much attracted to
merlins. There were two merlins [females] and four or five jacks [males], but
only Hugh's two jacks, *The Kahn* and *Nawab*, and one merlin would fly
ringers. We did a good deal of 'stooking' which is poor fun, to enter them.
We then went to the Downland where nearly all the larks were ringers. Here
we had some truly wonderful flights, and in my opinion I have seen very few
flights with peregrines to equal some of these. The cream of hawking

The Knights and friends at the Red Lion, Avebury, 1930.

On the downs at Avebury, 1933.

The merlin Ercles *on a lark, Avebury, 1933.*

undoubtedly – as far as this country goes – is Grouse hawking and Lark hawking, but unfortunately one cannot do both in the same year. There was a nest of hobbies on the downs, which got off, unmolested by the evil egg collectors. Four young and whenever we went there they used to come up and join in with our merlins, which was a nuisance, but at the same time showed us some very pretty flying, and on one occasion Norman's merlin chucked a ringer when a hobby appeared, the hobby continuing the flight – flying magnificently, and after several rings put the lark down and footed him high up in a terrific stoop. . . . I remained on with *The Khan* and *Nawab* for three more days and had some excellent flights, killing three or four larks a day with each. On the first of September I went down to Denne Hill to stay with Stanley and took the two jacks with me. I had a most enjoyable week. We shot partridges in the mornings and after lunch took the hawks over to Birchington where we had some splendid afternoons' hawking. The Knights' party motored over from Sevenoaks to join us on the last day and *Nawab* flew two of the most marvellous ringers and killed each time. The last flight could only be kept in view with glasses, and he killed in some trees about a mile downwind. This, I think, was the best flight I have ever seen either Grouse, Rook, Gull or Lark hawking. After a series of beautiful rings he fetched the lark almost out of sight of glasses and put him in a spinney with a tremendous long stoop, and it was a great piece of luck that Hugh and I found him pluming the lark in some undergrowth.

179

The Avebury meetings were soon to become the feature of the club year and were not restricted to lark hawking. Peregrines were flown at rooks and crows, goshawks at rabbits, and sparrowhawks were not forgotten. The membership continued to grow, including both the old well-known names and a goodly gathering of young enthusiasts. Major Stanley Allen continued to hawk the more difficult spring rooks from his lodge at Heytesbury, now with eyas peregrines, as Karl Mollen had given up at Valkenswaard. One Irish eyas tiercel, *Donegal*, proved an excellent hawk.

On one occasion this tiercel was lost, and found by two young boys living at Gore Cross, just north of Tilshead. When Stanley Allen arrived to recover his tiercel he found him in the copper boiler in the washhouse with a small boy sitting on the lid. Kept quiet and in the dark the tiercel was safe and undamaged, and Allen, much impressed with how the boys had managed, told one of them that he would make a good falconer. That small boy was Leonard Potter and, when once again Gilbert Blaine started grouse hawking in 1930, Leonard went with him as falconer, first to Altnaharra in Sutherland and in 1933 to Islay.

So once again falconry had a strong and enthusiastic following, with a club, the British Falconers' Club, playing a leading part in maintaining the future of 'Our Ancient Occupation'.

ye laste refuge!

Appendix

1872

Members
Lord Lilford
The Hon. C. Duncombe
Col Brooksbank
The Hon. G. Lascelles, Hon. Sec.
(incomplete list)
Falconers
John Barr
John Frost
Hawks
Barr's Hawks
2 Iceland gyrfalcons
Hydra eyas falcon
Miss Simmonds, eyas falcon
—, eyas falcon
Rothesay, eyas tiercel
—, passage tiercel
—, intermewed eyas falcon

Corbet's Hawks
The Rake, eyas tiercel
The Redman, eyas tiercel
Limerick, eyas tiercel
—, passage tiercel
—, Iceland falcon
—, Iceland tiercel

Fisher's Hawks
—, falcon
The Moor, tiercel
Score
23 rooks, 3 various
Total 26 head

1873

Members
(as above)
Falconers
(as above)
Hawks
The Empress, passage falcon, 1 year
Dutch Lady, passage falcon, 1 year
The Duck-killer, passage falcon,
    1 year
The Earl, passage tiercel, 1 year
The Doctor, passage tiercel,
    1 year
(incomplete list)
Score
132 rooks, 4 crows, 29 magpies,
    16 various
Total 181 head

1874

Members
The Earl of Craven
Lord Lilford
The Hon. G.R.C. Hill
The Hon. C. Duncombe
F.H. Salvin
A. Brooksbank
F. Newcome
The Hon. G. Lascelles, Hon. Sec.
Falconers
John Frost
Hawks
The Empress, passage falcon,
    2 years – 65 rooks
Pearl, passage falcon, 1 year
Turquoise, passage falcon, 1 year
Ruby, passage falcon, 1 year

Onyx, passage falcon, 1 year
The Major, passage tiercel, 1 year
Rocket, passage tiercel, 1 year
Coastguard, eyas tiercel, 1 year
The Duke, eyas tiercel, 1 year
Prince Charlie, eyas tiercel, young
Lowlander, eyas tiercel, young
Comet, eyas tiercel, young
Connaught, eyas tiercel, young
Medusa goshawk
Score
108 rooks, 1 crow, 5 magpies,
2 partridges, 30 rabbits,
4 various
Total 150 head

1875

Members
(As above)
Falconers
John Frost
Alfred Frost
Hawks
The Empress, passage falcon,
    3 years – 17 rooks
Pearl, passage falcon,
    2 years – 22 rooks
Turquoise, passage falcon, 2 years
Onyx, passage falcon, 2 years
Ruby, passage falcon, 2 years
Rowena, passage falcon,
    1 year – 11 rooks
Atlanta, passage falcon, 1 year
Formosa, passage falcon, 1 year
Sultana, passage falcon, 1 year
Minerva, passage falcon, 1 year
Diana, passage falcon,
    1 year – 4 rooks
Titania, passage falcon, 1 year
Bellona, passage falcon,
    1 year – 3 rooks
Score
54 rooks, 1 magpie, 1 partridge,

3 various
Total 59 head

1876

Members
Lord Lilford
The Earl of Craven
The Hon. C. Duncombe
The Hon. G.R.C. Hill
The Hon. Percy Wyndham
Capt. Brooksbank
F.H. Salvin
F. Newcome
The Hon. G. Lascelles, Hon. Sec.
Falconers
John Frost
Alfred Frost
Hawks
Pearl, passage falcon,
    3 years – 3 rooks
Rowena, passage falcon,
    2 years – 14 rooks
Regalia, passage falcon,
    1 year – 1 rook
Bois-le-duc, passage falcon,
    1 year – 60 rooks
Spinaway, passage falcon,
    1 year – 3 rooks
Pale Face, passage falcon, 1 year
Esmeralda, passage falcon,
    1 year – 43 rooks
Bandersnatch, passage falcon,
    1 year – 20 rooks
Chloe, passage falcon, 1 year
Boadicea, haggard falcon, 1 year
Castaway, haggard falcon, 1 year
The Flying Dutchman, passage
    tiercel, 1 year
Naaman, passage tiercel
Medusa, goshawk
Score
138 rooks, 4 crows, 2 partridges, 41

rabbits, 24 larks, 11 various
Total 220 head

1877

Members
Lord Lilford
The Hon. C. Duncombe
The Hon. G.R.C. Hill
The Hon. P. Wyndham
Capt Brooksbank
F. Newcome, Esq.
The Hon. G. Lascelles, Hon. Sec.
Falconers
John Frost
Alfred Frost
Hawks
Bois-le-duc, passage falcon,
    2 years – 44 rooks
Bandersnatch, passage falcon,
    2 years
Beeswing, passage falcon,
    1 year – 33 rooks
Wilbury, passage falcon,
    1 year – 27 rooks
Hebe, passage falcon,
    1 year – 1 rook
Cleopatra, passage falcon, 1 year
The Witch, passage falcon,
    1 year – 2 rooks
Penelope, passage falcon, 1 year
Juno, haggard falcon
Freya, Norwegian gyrfalcon, 1 year
Alladin (*Plenipotentiary*), passage
    tiercel, 1 year – 3 rooks
Snowdrop, passage tiercel, 1 year
Cabra, eyas falcon,
    1 year – 5 magpies
Jerry, eyas tiercel, 1 year – 3 magpies
Captain, eyas tiercel, 1 year
Yorkshire Relish, eyas tiercel, young
Elbana, eyas falcon, young
Erin, eyas falcon, young

Score
    108 rooks, 2 crows, 7 magpies,
    37 partridges, 112 rabbits,
    7 various
Total 273 head

1878

Members
Lord Lilford
The Hon. C. Dunscombe
The Hon. G. Hill
F. H. Salvin
F. Newcome, Esq.
Lord Londesborough
The Hon. G. Lascelles, Hon. Sec.
Falconers
John Frost
George Oxer
Hawks
Bois-le-duc, passage falcon, 3 years
Wilbury, passage falcon, 2 years
The Duchess, passage falcon, 1 year
Corsican Fairy, passage falcon,
    1 year
Boarding School Miss, passage
    falcon, 1 year
Harridan, passage falcon, 1 year
Maid of Honour, passage falcon,
    1 year
Erin, eyas falcon, 1 year
Cabra, eyas tiercel, 2 years
Yorkshire Relish, 1 year
Javelin, passage tiercel, 1 year
Adrian, haggard jerkin
—, passage goshawk
Medusa, goshawk, 5 years
Dreadnaught, eyas tiercel, young
Dauntless, eyas tiercel, young
Driver, eyas tiercel, young
John o'Groat, eyas tiercel, young
Captain, eyas tiercel, young
Northern Light, eyas falcon, young

Score
108 rooks, 6 crows, 20 magpies,
75 partridges, 6 rabbits, 29 larks,
20 various
Total 264 head

1879

Members
(as above)
Falconers
(as above)
Hawks
Bois-le-duc, passage falcon,
4 years – 28 rooks
Maid of Honour, passage falcon,
2 years
Amazon, passage falcon,
1 year – 27 rooks
Boomerang, passage falcon, 1 year
Wheel of Fortune, passage falcon,
1 year – 16 rooks
Hollandaise, passage falcon,
1 year – 4 rooks
Swiftsure, passage falcon, 1 year
Shooting Star, passage falcon,
1 year – 16 rooks
Princess, passage falcon,
1 year – 25 rooks
Queen of Sheba, passage falcon,
1 year
Northern Light, eyas falcon,
1 year – 5 rooks
Cabra, eyas tiercel, 3 years
Dreadnaught, eyas tiercel, 1 year
Dauntless, eyas tiercel, 1 year
Driver, eyas tiercel, 1 year
Sailor, eyas tiercel, 1 year
John o'Groat, eyas tiercel, 1 year
Elbana, eyas falcon,
2 years – 4 rooks
Medusa, goshawk, 7 years
Morna, eyas falcon, young

Buccaneer, eyas tiercel, young
Bushranger, eyas tiercel, young
Meteor, eyas tiercel, young
Mercury, eyas tiercel, young
Score
125 rooks, 1 crow, 3 curlew, 13
magpies, 3 various, 41 partridges
48 magpies, 27 rooks, 3 pheasant,
4 various
Total 268 head

1880

Members
(as above)
Falconers
(as above)
Hawks
Bois-le-duc, passage falcon,
5 years – 5 rooks
Princess, passage falcon,
2 years – 13 rooks
Azrael, passage falcon,
1 year – 7 rooks
Bonnibell, passage falcon, 1 year
Makeshift, passage falcon,
1 year – 27 rooks
Satanella, passage falcon, 1 year
Enchantress, passage falcon, 1 year
Guinevere, passage falcon,
1 year – 1 rook
Cockatrice, passage falcon,
1 year – 16 rooks
Virago, passage falcon, 1 year
Catapult, passage falcon, 1 year
Candace, passage falcon,
1 year – 5 rooks
Score
97 rooks, 50 magpies, 56 partridges,
4 pheasants, 8 various
Total 215 head

1881

Members
(as above)
Falconers
(as above)
Hawks
Candace, passage falcon,
    2 years – 24 rooks
Amesbury, passage falcon,
    1 year – 39 rooks
Heroine, passage falcon,
    1 year – 9 rooks
Myra, passage falcon,
    1 year – 12 rooks
Morgiana, passage falcon,
    1 year – 3 rooks
Capsicum, passage falcon,
    1 year – 3 rooks
Termagant, passage falcon, 1 year
Gitana, passage falcon,
    1 year – 49 rooks
Mrs Bagot, eyas falcon, 1 year
Rifleman, eyas tiercel, 1 year
Sharpshooter, eyas tiercel, 1 year
—, Haggard goshawk
Aide de Camp, eyas tiercel, 1 year
Creole, eyas falcon, 1 year
Parachute, eyas falcon, young
Score
150 rooks, 128 partridges,
    7 pheasants, 2 crows, 39 rabbits,
    2 wild duck, 19 magpies, 7 various
Total 354 head

1882

Members
(as above)
Falconers
(as above)
Hawks
Candace, passage falcon, 3 years

Amesbury, passage falcon,
    2 years – 31 rooks
Gitana, passage falcon,
    2 years – 21 rooks
Olivette, passage falcon,
    1 year – 24 rooks
Patience, passage falcon,
    1 year – 5 rooks
Lady Jane, passage falcon,
    1 year – 9 rooks
White Lady, passage falcon,
    1 year – 39 rooks
Angela, passage falcon,
    1 year – 6 rooks, 36 grouse
Griselda, passage falcon,
    1 year – 43 rooks
Manola, passage falcon,
    1 year – 2 rooks
The Rogue, passage falcon, 1 year
Parachute, eyas falcon,
    1 year – 138 grouse/partridge
Valterie, eyas falcon, 1 year
Vanquisher, eyas tiercel, 1 year
Peter, eyas tiercel, 1 year
Creole, eyas falcon,
    2 years – 10 grouse
Belfry, eyas tiercel,
    1 year – 3 grouse
Black Prince, eyas tiercel, 1 year
Vesta, eyas falcon,
    young – 62 grouse/partridge
Aide de Camp, eyas tiercel,
    2 years – 25 grouse/partridge
Score
180 rooks, 6 crows, 40 magpies,
    3 curlew, 200 grouse, 185
    partridges, 6 pheasants, 5 hares,
    25 rabbits, 21 various
Total 671 head

1883

Members
Lord Lilford

Appendix

Colonel Brooksbank
F.H. Salvin
W. St Quintin
Lord Londesborough
B. Heywood Jones
P. Hambro, Esq.
The Hon. G. Lascelles, Hon. Sec.
Hon. Members
The Hon. C. Duncombe
The Hon. G.R.C. Hill
Falconers
John Frost
Hawks
Amesbury passage falcon,
   3 years – 11 rooks
Olivette, passage falcon,
   2 years – 11 rooks
Lady Jane, passage falcon,
   2 years – 10 rooks
Iolanthe, passage falcon
   1 year – 45 rooks
Alberta, passage falcon,
   1 year – 36 rooks
Alda, passage falcon,
   1 year – 21 rooks
Arethusa, passage falcon,
   1 year – 47 rooks
Dulcibella, passage falcon,
   1 year – 25 rooks
Stella, passage falcon,
   1 year – 6 rooks
Shotover, passage falcon,
   1 year – 1 rook
Dynamite, eyas falcon,
   young – 42 grouse, 54 partridges
Vesta, eyas falcon,
   2 years – 42 grouse
Virginia, eyas falcon,
   2 years – 3 grouse
Romulus, eyas tiercel,
   2 years – 3 grouse, 3 partridges
Forester, eyas tiercel,
   young – 23 partridges
Sheriff, eyas tiercel,

young – 21 partridges
Score
204 rooks, 8 crows, 1 jackdaw,
   8 curlew, 40 magpies, 85 grouse,
   7 blackgrouse, 87 partridges,
   3 pheasants, 21 various
Total 464 head

1884

Members
(as above)
Falconers
(as above)
Hawks
Iolanthe, passage falcon,
   2 years – 30 rooks
Alberta, passage falcon,
   2 years – 19 rooks
Sybil, passage falcon,
   1 year – 17 rooks
Clarice, passage falcon, 1 year
Theresa, passage falcon,
   1 year – 13 rooks, 16 grouse
Falka, passage falcon,
   1 year – 27 rooks
Galatea, passage falcon,
   1 year – 3 rooks
Belinda, passage falcon,
   1 year – 10 rooks, 5 grouse
Catamaran, passage falcon,
   1 year – 5 rooks
Dulcibella, passage falcon,
   2 years – 2 rooks
Vesta, eyas falcon,
   3 years – 34 grouse
Forester, eyas tiercel,
   1 year – 2 magpies
The Sheriff, eyas tiercel,
   1 year – 6 magpies
Destiny, passage tiercel
   –6 grouse, 5 magpies
Detective, tiercel – 5 magpies

David, tiercel – 8 magpies
Sorcerer, eyas tiercel – 2 grouse
Dashaway, eyas tiercel – 4 grouse
Discord, eyas falcon – 1 grouse
Dynamite, eyas falcon,
   1 year – 34 grouse
Eclipse, eyas falcon,
   young – 4 grouse
Coralic, eyas falcon,
   young – 9 grouse
Express, eyas tiercel,
   young – 11 grouse
Score
123 rooks, 23 magpies, 2 jackdaws,
   156 grouse, 5 blackgrouse, 85
   partridges, 10 pheasants, 2 snipe,
   77 rabbits, 31 various
Total 515 head

1885

Members
Lord Lilford
F. Newcome
W.H. St Quintin
Lord Londesborough
B. Heywood Jones
P. Hambro, Esq.
Duke of St Albans
Duke of Portland
E.W. Portman
The Hon. G. Lascelles, Hon.Sec
Falconers
John Frost
George Oxer
Ernest Kitchener
Hawks
Falka, passage falcon,
   2 years – 13 rooks
Sybil, passage falcon,
   2 years – 27 rooks, 22 grouse
Sylvia, haggard falcon – 39 rooks
Almida, passage falcon,
   1 year – 27 rooks

Elgiva, passage falcon,
   1 year – 18 rooks
Camilla, passage falcon,
   1 year – 33 rooks
Carmen, passage falcon,
   1 year – 14 rooks
Nadine, passage falcon,
   1 year – 22 rooks
Clarissa, passage falcon,
   1 year – 1 rook
Her Grace, passage falcon,
   1 year – 7 rooks
Vesta, eyas falcon,
   4 years – 31 grouse
Sorcerer, eyas tiercel, 1 year
Destiny, passage tiercel,
   2 years – 22 magpies and various
David, eyas tiercel,
   2 years – 10 magpies and various
Score
186 rooks, 19 magpies, 71 grouse,
   105 partridges, 20 pheasants,
   134 rabbits, 46 various
Total 581 head

1886

Members
Lord Lilford
F. Newcome
W.H. St Quintin
Lord Londesborough
B. Heywood Jones
Duke of St Albans
Duke of Portland
E.W. Portman
Revd W. Newcome
The Hon. G. Lascelles, Hon.Sec.
Hon. Members
The Hon. C. Duncombe
The Hon. G.R. Hill
Colonel Brooksbank
F.H. Salvin, Esq.

Falconers
John Frost
E. Kitchener
Hawks
Nadine, passage falcon,
   2 years – 20 rooks, 7 grouse
Camilla, passage falcon,
   2 years – 40 rooks
Her Grace, passage falcon,
   2 years – 21 rooks
Bacchante, haggard falcon –
   31 rooks, 14 grouse
Stopgap, haggard falcon – 3 rooks
Marjory, passage falcon,
   1 year – 24 rooks
Clochette, passage falcon,
   1 year – 1 rook
Elsa, passage falcon,
   1 year – 48 rooks
—, passage falcon, 1 year
Vesta, eyas falcon,
   5 years – 31 grouse
Paradox, eyas tiercel, 1 year
Moonraker, eyas, 1 year
David, eyas tiercel, 3 years
Fleetwing, eyas falcon – 24 grouse
Paragon, eyas tiercel, young –
   11 grouse
Christopher, eyas tiercel,
   young – 9 grouse
Score
167 rooks, 8 magpies, 11 curlews,
   97 grouse, 46 partridges,
   15 pheasants, 112 rabbits,
   27 various
Total 483 head

1887

Members
(as above)
Hawks
Elsa, passage falcon,

   2 years – 46 rooks, 28 grouse
Marjorie, passage falcon,
   2 years – 23 rooks
Marpessa haggard falcon – 20 rooks
Farthingale, passage falcon –
   23 rooks
Ragazza, passage falcon, 1 year
Lucetta, passage falcon,
   1 year – 25 rooks, 2 grouse
Bessy Bedlam, passage falcon,
   1 year – 35 rooks
Queen of Trumps, passage falcon,
   1 year
Lady Wildair, passage falcon,
   1 year – 27 rooks, 13 grouse
Shuttlecock, passage falcon, 1 year
Vesta, eyas falcon,
   6 years – 40 grouse
Destiny, passage tiercel, 4 years
Daniels, passage tiercel, 1 year
Cymba, falcon – 14 rooks
Handa, eyas falcon, young –
   6 grouse
Hermes, tiercel
Hero, tiercel
Score
209 rooks, 13 magpies, 95 grouse,
   2 blackgame, 5 pheasants, 114
   partridges, 112 rabbits, 26 various
Total 576 head

1888

Members
(as above)
Falconers
(as above)
Hawks
Elsa, passage falcon,
   3 years – 42 rooks, 26 grouse
Lady Wildair, passage falcon,
   2 years – 16 rooks, 21 grouse
Bessie Bedlam, passage falcon,
   2 years – 34 rooks, 4 grouse

Farthingale, passage falcon,
    2 years – 31 rooks and curlew
Handmaid, passage falcon,
    1 year – 1 rook
Maruja, passage falcon,
    1 year – 8 rooks
Fortune, passage falcon, 1 year
Gwendoline, passage falcon.
    1 year – 2 rooks
Dorothy, passage falcon,
    1 year – 25 rooks
Seaweed, passage falcon,
    1 year – 26 rooks
Miriam, passage falcon,
    1 year – 3 rooks
Destiny, passage tiercel, 5 years
Vesta, eyas falcon,
    7 years – 28 grouse
Stumpy, eyas tiercel, 1 year
Score
189 rooks and crows, 84 grouse, 1
    greyhen, 21 partridges,
    3 pheasants, 225 rabbits,
    12 various
Total 526 head

1889

Members
(as above)
Falconers
John Frost
Joe Stone
Hawks
Elsa, passage falcon,
    4 years – 15 rooks, 38 grouse
Dorothy, passage falcon,
    2 years – 8 rooks
Seaweed, passage falcon,
    2 years – 15 rooks, 19 grouse
Coquette, passage falcon,
    1 year – 24 rooks
Frailty, passage falcon,

1 year – 7 rooks
Castanette, passage falcon,
    1 year – 29 rooks
Leda, passage falcon,
    1 year – 10 grouse
Matilda, passage falcon,
    1 year – 15 rooks
Celia, passage falcon,
    1 year – 22 rooks
Petticoat, passage falcon,
    1 year – 7 rooks
Vesta, eyas falcon,
    8 years – 27 grouse
Random, passage tiercel, 1 year
Forester, passage tiercel, 1 year
The Shahin – 8 grouse
Score
135 rooks, 8 magpies, 6 curlew,
    105 grouse, (incomplete)

1890

Members
(as above)
Falconers
(as above)
Hawks
Elsa, passage falcon,
    5 years – 35 rooks, 31 grouse
Seaweed, passage falcon,
    3 years – 6 rooks
Matilda, passage falcon,
    2 years – 1 rook
Castanette, passage falcon, 2 years
Burlesque, passage falcon,
    1 year – 57 rooks
Jasmine, passage falcon,
    1 year – 22 rooks
Evadne, passage falcon,
    1 year – 43 rooks
Ursula, passage falcon,
    1 year – 43 rooks, 31 grouse
Glauca, passage falcon,

1 year – 21 rooks
Ustane, passage falcon,
   1 year – 17 rooks
Dagonet, passage tiercel, 1 year
Bollinger, passage tiercel, 1 year
The Shahin
Vesta, eyas falcon,
   9 years – 18 grouse
Handa, eyas falcon,
   1 year – 15 grouse
Score
242 rooks, 1 jackdaw, 1 crow,
   2 curlew, 3 magpies, 95 grouse,
   (incomplete)

1891

Members
Lord Lilford
F. Newcome
W.H. St Quintin
Lord Londesborough
B. Heywood Jones
Duke of Portland
E.W. Portman
Revd W. Newcome
The Hon. G. Lascelles, Hon. Sec.
Col. Watson
A. Newall
Falconers
George Oxer
Hawks
Elsa, passage falcon,
   6 years – 3 grouse
Glauca, passage falcon,
   2 years – 21 rooks
Evadne, passage falcon
   2 years – 11 rooks
Ursula, passage falcon,
   2 years – 50 rooks, 25 grouse
Clinkerina, passage falcon,
   1 year – 15 rooks
Letty Lind, passage falcon,
   1 year – 18 rooks

Phyllis, passage falcon,
   1 year – 18 rooks
Mermaid, passage falcon,
   1 year – 14 rooks
Fleetwing, passage falcon,
   1 year – 2 rooks, 10 grouse
Irish, eyas falcon – 4 grouse
Score
146 rooks, 2 crows, 53 grouse,
   16 partridges, 17 gulls,
   (incomplete)

1892

Members
Lord Lilford
Revd W. Newcome
F. Newcome
W.H. St Quintin
Earl of Londesborough
B. Heywood Jones
Duke of Portland
The Hon. E.W.B. Portman
Col. Watson
A. Newall
The Hon. G. Lascelles, Hon. Sec.
Hon. Members
The Hon. C. Duncombe
Col. Brooksbank
F.H. Salvin
Capt. S. Biddulph
Falconers
George Oxer
Reg Moore
Hawks
Ursula, passage falcon,
   3 years – 20 rooks, 21 grouse
Glauca, passage falcon,
   3 years – 3 rooks
Phyllis, passage falcon,
   2 years – 2 rooks, 13 grouse
Letty Lind, passage falcon,
   2 years – 5 rooks

Olinda, passage falcon
  1 year – 17 rooks
Cinderella, passage falcon,
  1 year – 34 rooks
Sweetmeat, passage falcon, 1 year
Seabreeze, passage falcon,
  1 year – 15 rooks
Beatrice, passage falcon,
  1 year – 17 rooks
Mabel, passage falcon,
  1 year – 1 rook
Swiftsure, passage falcon,
  1 year – 12 rooks
Ianthe, haggard falcon – 1 rook
Seaweed, 2 rooks, 5 grouse
Agatha, eyas falcon – 34 grouse
Score
129 rooks and crows, 74 grouse
  (incomplete)

4 years – 1 rook, 18 grouse
Olinda, passage falcon,
  2 years – 2 rooks
Beatrice, passage falcon, 2 years
Danceaway, passage falcon,
  1 year – 60 rooks
The Midget, passage falcon,
  1 year – 49 rooks, 14 grouse
Hilda, passage falcon,
  1 year – 3 rooks
Rosalba, passage falcon,
  1 year – 39 rooks
Patricia, haggard falcon – 7 rooks,
  9 grouse
Pride of Scamptston, haggard
  falcon – 5 rooks, 5 grouse
(incomplete list)
Score
166 rooks and crows, 68 grouse,
  (incomplete list)

1893

Members
Lord Lilford
Revd W. Newcome
F. Newcome
W.H. St Quintin
B. Heywood Jones
Duke of Portland
The Hon. E.W.B. Portman
Col. Watson
A. Newall
The Hon. G. Lascelles, Hon. Sec.
Hon. Members
The Hon. C. Dunscombe
Col. Brooksbank
F.H. Salvin
Capt. S. Biddulph
Earl of Londesborough
Falconers
(as above)
Hawks
Ursula, passage falcon,

1894

Members
(as above)
Falconers
(as above)
Hawks
Danceaway, passage falcon,
  2 years – 54 rooks
Midget, passage falcon,
  2 years – 9 rooks
Rosalba, passage falcon,
  2 years – 15 rooks
Jannette, passage falcon,
  1 year – 42 rooks
Irene, passage falcon,
  1 year – 4 rooks
Marcia, passage falcon,
  1 year – 4 rooks
Whirlwind, passage falcon, 1 year
Pauline, haggard falcon – 21 rooks
—, eyas falcon, 1 year – 2 rooks

Appendix

(incomplete list)
Score
150 rooks, 2 curlews (incomplete list)

1895

Members
Lord Lilford
Revd W. Newcome
F. Newcome
W.H. St Quintin
B. Heywood Jones
Duke of Portland
The Hon. E.W.B. Portman
Col. Watson
J. Fowler
W.M. Clarke
The Hon. G. Lascelles, Hon. Sec.
Falconers
(as above)
Hawks
Danceaway, passage falcon,
    3 years – 49 rooks
Jannette, passage falcon, 2 years
Marcia, passage falcon, 2 years
Caprice, passage falcon, 1 year
Yvette, passage falcon, 1 year
Ulrica, passage falcon, 1 year
Nerissa, passage falcon, 1 year
Daisy, passage falcon, 1 year
Eva, passage falcon, 1 year
Elaine, passage falcon, 1 year
Babette, passage falcon, 1 year
Termagant, passage falcon, 1 year
Patience, eyas falcon,
    1 year – 64 partridges
Osman, eyas tiercel,
    2 years – 38 partridges
Score
154 rooks
(incomplete)

1896

Members
Lord Lilford
F. Newcome
Revd W. Newcome
W.H. St Quintin
B. Heywood Jones
Duke of Portland
Col. Watson
J.E. Harting
W.M. Clarke
J.H. Fowler
W. Duncome
The Hon. G. Lascelles, Hon. Sec.
Hon. Members
The Hon. C. Duncombe
Col. Brooksbank
F.H. Salvin
Capt. S. Biddulph
Earl of Londesborough
Falconers
George Oxer
John Frost
Hawks
Danceaway, passage falcon,
    4 years – 50 rooks
Yvette, passage falcon,
    2 years – 7 rooks
Nerissa, passage falcon,
    2 years – 6 rooks
Winifred, passage falcon,
    1 year – 40 rooks
Eileen, passage falcon,
    1 year – 25 rooks
Sheila, passage falcon,
    1 year – 28 rooks
Trilby, passage falcon
    1 year – 27 rooks
Edith, passage falcon, 1 year
Amanda, passage falcon, 1 year
Switchback, eyas
Siegfried, eyas tiercel –
    49 partridges
Siegmund, eyas tiercel – 1 partridge

Patience, eyas falcon,
   2 years – 32 partridges
Score
180 rooks, 3 crows, 82 partridges,
   3 various

1897

Members
(as above, minus Lord Lilford plus
   E. Meade-Waldo)
Falconers
(as above)
Hawks
Danceaway, passage falcon,
   5 years – 38 rooks
Winifred, passage falcon,
   2 years – 30 rooks
Eileen, passage falcon
   2 years – 5 rooks
Osra, passage falcon,
   1 year – 70 rooks
Ancilla, passage falcon,
   1 year – 3 rooks
Daphne, passage falcon, 1 year
Victress, passage falcon,
   1 year – 17 rooks
Indeth, passage falcon, 1 year
Lufra, haggard falcon – 11 rooks
Persimmon, eyas tiercel,
   young – 80 partridges
Patience, eyas falcon,
   3 years – 64 partridges
Thais, eyas – 14 partridges
Galtee More, eyas – 10 partridges
Score
171 rooks, 3 crows, 172 partridges,
   12 various

1898

Members
F. Newcome, Esq.

W.H. St Quintin
B. Heywood Jones
Duke of Portland
Col. Watson
J.E. Harting, Esq.
W.M. Clarke, Esq.
J.H. Fowler, Esq.
W. Duncombe, Esq.
E. Meade-Waldo
R. Corbet, Esq.
E. Hare, Esq.
A. Chance, Esq.
The Hon. G. Lascelles, Hon. Sec.
Hon. Members
(as above)
Falconers
(as above)
Hawks
Danceaway, passage falcon,
   6 years – 25 rooks
Osra, passage falcon,
   2 years – 16 rooks
Ancilla, passage falcon, 2 years
Draculla, passage falcon
   1 year – 29 rooks
Chloe, passage falcon,
   1 year – 2 rooks
Actress, passage falcon, 1 year
Paramount, passage falcon,
   1 year – 35 rooks
Bonnylass, passage falcon,
   1 year – 14 rooks
Badalia, passage falcon, 1 year
Thais, eyas falcon, 1 year
Persimmon, eyas tiercel, 1 year
Score
114 rooks, 7 crows, 8 magpies,
   (incomplete)

1899

Members
(as above, plus N. Heywood)

193

Falconers
George Oxer
Robert Slightam
Hawks
Danceaway, passage falcon,
   7 years – 12 rooks
Paramount, passage falcon, 2 years
Chloe, passage falcon,
   2 years – 1 rook
Camarine, passage falcon,
   1 year – 56 rooks
Modesty, passage falcon,
   1 year – 11 rooks
Minette, passage falcon,
   1 year – 10 rooks
Tragedy, passage falcon, 1 year
Althea, passage falcon, 1 year
Victress, passage falcon,
   1 year – 7 rooks
Elvira, passage falcon,
   1 year – 49 rooks
Banshee, eyas falcon, 2 years
Persimmon, eyas tiercel, 3 years
Gimcrack, eyas tiercel, 2 years
Gulliver, eyas tiercel, 2 years
Score
138 rooks, 5 crows, 1 jackdaw,
   4 magpies, 1 curlew

1900

Members
(as above)
Falconers
(as above)
Hawks
Elvira, passage falcon,
   2 years – 41 rooks
Camarine, passage falcon,
   2 years – 3 rooks
Saucy Puss, passage falcon,
   1 year – 47 rooks
Vedette, passage falcon,
   1 year – 6 rooks

Coraline, passage falcon,
   1 year – 1 rook
Agnes, passage falcon,
   1 year – 36 rooks
Gulliver, eyas tiercel, 3 years
Mr Wardell, eyas tiercel, 1 year
Score
132 rooks, 1 crow, 12 magpies,
   (incomplete)

1901

Members
(as above, minus A. Chance and
   The Duke of Portland)
Falconers
(as above)
Hawks
Elvira, passage falcon, 3 years
Saucy Puss, passage falcon,
   2 years – 27 rooks
Agnes, passage falcon,
   2 years – 3 rooks
Shelagh, haggard Falcon – 54 rooks
Black Jane, passage falcon, 1 year
Algitha, passage falcon, 1 year
Fury, passage falcon,
   1 year – 47 rooks
Amenda, passage falcon,
   1 year – 3 rooks
Lady Husheen, passage falcon,
   1 year
Quadroon, eyas falcon, 1 year
A Barbary tiercel
G. Blaine's tiercel
St Quintin's tiercel
Mr Wardell's tiercel
Score
126 rooks, 7 crows, 20 magpies,
   3 curlews, 77 partridges

1902

Members
W.H. St Quintin, Esq.
B. Heywood Jones, Esq.
J.H. Fowler, Esq., MD
N. Heywood, Esq.
Earl of Sefton
Capt. Noble
C. Garnett, Esq.
The Hon. G. Lascelles, Hon. Sec.
Subscribers
W. Duncombe, Esq.
R. Heywood, Esq.
H. Talbot, Esq.
G. Thursby, Esq.
G. Wardle, Esq.
E.B. Michell, Esq.
Hon. Members
F.H. Salvin
Col. Brooksbank
Capt. S. Biddulph
F. Newcome
Falconers
(as above)
Hawks
Shelagh, haggard falcon,
  2 years – 62 rooks
Algitha, passage falcon,
  2 years – 4 rooks
Fury, passage falcon,
  2 years – 9 rooks
Sufra, passage falcon,
  1 year – 9 rooks
Creeping Jane, passage falcon,
  1 year – 24 rooks
Philippa, passage falcon,
  1 year –30 rooks
Caroline, passage falcon,
  1 year – 2 rooks
Samia, passage falcon, 1 year
Caterona, eyas falcon, 2 years
Roderick, passage tiercel, 1 year
Random, passage tiercel, 1 year
The Major, eyas tiercel, 1 year

Score
125 rooks, 8 crows, 24 magpies,
  3 curlews, 1 peewit,
  1 woodpigeon (incomplete)

1903

Members
(as above, plus E. Hare and
  W.M. Clarke)
Falconers
(as above)
Hawks
Shelagh, haggard falcon,
  3 years – 7 rooks
Philippa, passage falcon,
  2 years – 33 rooks
Clementine, passage falcon, 1 year
Gilda, passsage falcon,
  1 year – 4 rooks
Hermione, passage falcon,
  1 year – 3 rooks
Josephine, passage falcon,
  1 year – 57 rooks
Ethel, passage falcon, 1 year
Brenda, passage falcon,
  1 year – 13 rooks
Roderick, passage tiercel, 2 years
Mauser, passage tiercel, 1 year
Mannlicher, passage tiercel, 1 year
Haggard tiercel
Score
112 rooks, 5 crows, 8 magpies,
  3 curlews, 1 jackdaw,
  (incomplete)

1904

Members
(as above)
Falconers
(as above)

Hawks
Philippa, passage falcon,
   3 years – 17 rooks
Brenda, passage falcon,
   2 years – 14 rooks
Josephine, passage falcon,
   2 years – 61 rooks
Little Mary, passage falcon,
   1 year – 19 rooks
Rosemary, passage falcon,
   1 year – 17 rooks
Alruna, passage falcon,
   1 year – 12 rooks
Damsel, passage falcon, 1 year
Edna, passage falcon,
   1 year – 1 rook
Mannlicher, passage tiercel, 2 years
Rupert, passage tiercel, 1 year
Rattler, passage tiercel, 1 year
Robin, passage tiercel, 1 year
Rachel, eyas falcon, 1 year
Roseberry, eyas tiercel, 1 year
Score
134 rooks, 5 crows, 1 jackdaw,
   5 magpies, 42 partridges, 28 gulls
   (incomplete)

1905

Members
(not known)
Falconers
(as above)
Hawks
Josephine, passage falcon,
   3 years – 44 rooks
Brenda, passage falcon,
   3 years – 6 rooks
Rosemary, passage falcon,
   2 years – 4 rooks
Aimwell, passage falcon,
   1 year – 72 rooks
Margot, passage falcon,
   1 year – 58 rooks

Madge, passage falcon,
   1 year – 9 rooks
Rance, passage falcon, 1 year
Charybdis, passage falcon,
   1 year – 20 rooks
Scylla, passage falcon,
   1 year – 5 rooks
Gladys, falcon – 1 rook
Rattler, passage tiercel,
   2 years – 1 magpie
Score
204 rooks, 18 crows, 1 jackdaw,
   5 magpies
   Total 224 head (incomplete)

1906

Members
(not known)
Falconers
(as above)
Hawks
Josephine, passage falcon, 4 years
Aimwell, passage falcon, 2 years
Margot, passage falcon, 2 years
Eva, passage falcon, 1 year
Lucretia, passage falcon, 1 year
Ruby, passage falcon, 1 year
Patricia, passage falcon, 1 year
Stella, passage falcon, 1 year
Auguste, eyas tiercel, 1 year
Pierre, passage tiercel, 1 year
Amedee, passage tiercel, 1 year
Monkton, eyas tiercel, young
Avebury, eyas tiercel, young
Vasterne, eyas tiercel, young
Scylla, passage falcon, 2 years
Psyche, passage falcon, 1 year
Vengeance, tiercel, 1 year
Lundy, eyas tiercel, 1 year
Score(not known)

1907

Members
(not known)
Falconers
(as above)
Hawks
Aimwell, passage falcon,
   3 years – 36 rooks
Margot, passage falcon, 3 years
Ruby, passage falcon, 2 years
Clairette, passage falcon,
   1 year – 63 rooks
Nina, passage falcon, 1 year
Viola, passage falcon, 1 year
Jocasta, passage falcon, 1 year
Armorel, passage falcon, 1 year
Pierre, passage tiercel, 2 years
Amedee, passage tiercel, 2 years
Blaine's, tiercel
Monkton, eyas tiercel, 1 year
Silbury, eyas tiercel
Cherhill, eyas tiercel
Score
154 rooks

1908

Members
(not known)
Falconers
(as above)
Hawks
Clairette, passage falcon, 2 years
Nina, passage falcon, 2 years
Jocasta, passage falcon, 2 years
Portia, haggard falcon
Heroine, passage falcon, 1 year
Iris, passage falcon, 1 year
Novice, passage falcon, 1 year
Audry, passage falcon, 1 year
Spitfire, passage falcon, 1 year
Noor Khan, passage falcon, 1 year
Silbury, eyas tiercel, 1 year

Manton, eyas tiercel, young
Glory Ann, eyas falcon,
   young – 15 partridges
Mary Ann, eyas falcon,
   young – 31 partridges
Overton, eyas tiercel, young
Kennet, eyas tiercel, young
Score
(not known)

1909

Members
(not known)
Falconers
(as above)
Hawks
Georgette, passage falcon, 1 year
Wendy, passage falcon, 1 year
Spitfire, passage falcon, 2 years
Vera, passage falcon, 1 year
Blaine's falcon
Glory Ann, eyas falcon,
   1 year – 20 partridges
Noor Khan, passage falcon, 2 years
Victress, eyas falcon,
   2 years – 26 partridges
Salome, eyas falcon,
   young – 26 partridges
Maud Allan, eyas falcon,
   young – 5 partridges
Score
(not known)

1910

Members
(not known)
Falconers
(as above)
Hawks

Appendix

Lorna, haggard falcon
Carlotta, passage falcon, 1 year
Althia, passage falcon, 1 year
Beryl, passage falcon, 1 year
Doris, passage falcon, 1 year
Iris, passage falcon, 1 year
Annabel, passage falcon, 1 year
Salome, eyas falcon, 1 year
Evelyn, eyas falcon,
    young – 45 partridges
Cuckoo, eyas falcon,
    young – 6 partridges
Lemburg, eyas tiercel,
    young – 33 partridges
Puck, eyas tiercel,
    young – 30 partridges
Score
137 partridges
(incomplete)

1911

Members
(not known)
Falconers
(as above)
Hawks
Cicely, falcon
Althia, passage falcon, 2 years
Kurringunda, passage falcon, 1 year
Sylph, passage falcon, 1 year
Anita, passage falcon, 1 year
Glenmora
Salome, eyas falcon, 2 years
Evelyn, eyas falcon,
    2 years – 11 partridges
Puck, eyas tiercel,
    2 years – 15 partridges
Rex, eyas tiercel,
    young – 23 partridges
Crippin, eyas tiercel,
    young – 4 partridges

Score
125 partridges
(incomplete)

1912

Members
(not known)
Falconers
(as above)
Hawks
Sylph, passage falcon, 2 years
Kurringunda, passage falcon,
    2 years
Flavia, passage falcon, 1 year
Esperanza, passage falcon, 1 year
Glenmora, falcon, 2 years
Helga, falcon, 2 years
Rex, tiercel
Score
At Aintree Club hawks killed
29 gulls, 59 partridges,
(total score not known)

1913

Members
(not known)
Falconers
(as above)
Hawks
Delphine, passage falcon, 1 year
Helga, falcon, 3 years
Wildfire, passage falcon, 1 year
Olivia, passage falcon, 1 year
Esperanza, passage falcon, 2 years
Puck, eyas tiercel,
    4 years – 8 partridges
Rex, eyas tiercel,
    2 years – 12 partridges
Zena, eyas falcon,
    1 year – 11 partridges

Eve, eyas falcon,
    young – 20 partridges
Emma, eyas falcon,
    young – 10 partridges
Carol, eyas tiercel,
    1 year – 15 partridges
Stroma, falcon from Blaine
Score
(not known)

1914

Members
(not known)
Falconers
George Oxer
Ben Bessant
Hawks
Delphine, passage falcon, 2 years
Rosalind, passage falcon, 1 year
Cleone, passage falcon, 1 year
Timandra, passage falcon, 1 year
Sister B, passage falcon, 1 year
Melesandre, haggard falcon
Score
(not known)

1920

Members
(not known)
Hon. Sec. and Manager
The Hon. G. Blaine
Falconers
Richard Best
Ted Woods
Hawks
Lady Jane, passage falcon, 1 year
Destiny, passage falcon, 1 year
White Wings, passage falcon, 1 year
Alsace, passage falcon, 1 year

Score
Over 65 rooks

1921

Members
C. Garnett, Esq.
Major S. Allen
Captain K. Palmer
Gilbert Blaine, Hon. Sec.
(incomplete list)
Falconers
R. Best
E. Woods
G. Blake
Hawks
Blaine's Hawks
Titania, passage falcon – 31 rooks
Mary Rose, passage falcon
    – 43 rooks
Quanza, passage falcon – 13 rooks
Ruth, passage falcon – 1 rook
Dawn, haggard falcon – 57 rooks
Lady Jane, passage falcon,
    2 years – 37 rooks
White Wings, passage falcon,
    2 years – 1 rook
  Allen's Hawks
Destiny, passage falcon,
    2 years – 2 rooks
Ishante, haggard falcon
Score
188 rooks

1922

Members
(as above)
Falconers
(as above)
Hawks
Blaine's Hawks

Lady Jane, passage falcon,
   3 years – 2 rooks
Mary Rose, passage falcon,
   2 years – 17 rooks
Ariadne, haggard falcon – 7 rooks
Rhoda, passage falcon – 1 rook

Palmer's Hawks
Christmas, eyas falcon – 14 rooks
Miranda, passage falcon – 27 rooks
Lavinia, passage falcon – 18 rooks

Allen's Hawk
Princess, passage falcon – 12 rooks
Score
98 rooks

1923

Members
(as above)
Falconers
(as above)
Hawks
Blaine's Hawks
Ariadne, haggard falcon,
   2 years – 10 rooks
Simond's Hawk
Althaea, passage falcon – 13 rooks

Langford's Hawk
Diana, passage falcon – 1 rook

Palmer's Hawk
— , passage falcon – ½ rook

Allen's Hawk
Christmas, eyas falcon,
   2 years – 1½ rooks
Score
26 rooks

1924

Members
(as above)
Falconers
(as above)
Hawks
Phoebe, passage falcon,
   3 years – 2 rooks
Piga, eyas falcon – 14½ rooks
Agrippa, haggard falcon – 8 rooks
Blue Foot, passage falcon
Yellow Foot, passage falcon – 7 rooks
Nydia, passage falcon – 14½ rooks
Donegal, passage falcon – 8 rooks
Score
54 rooks

1925

Members
Major S. Allen
Captain K. Palmer
George Blackall Simonds
C.W. Garnett
Gilbert Blaine, Hon. Sec.
Subscribers
Captain Blew Jones
Mr Pye
(incomplete)
Falconers
(as above)
Hawks
Flying Duchess, haggard falcon
   – 4 rooks
Hurrybelle, passage falcon
   – 26 rooks
Lancia, passage falcon – 25 rooks
Romola, passage falcon – 6 rooks
Primrose, passage falcon – 24 rooks
Judith, passage falcon – 4 rooks
Fleur, passage falcon
Xantippe, haggard falcon – 5 rooks

Score
94 rooks

1926

Members
(as above)
Falconers
(as above)
Hawks
Hurrybelle, passage falcon
    2 years – 5 rooks
Lancia, passage falcon
    2 years – 4 rooks
Primrose, passage falcon,
    2 years – 21 rooks
Augusta, haggard falcon – 10 rooks
Beeswing, passage falcon – 10 rooks

Andromeda, passage falcon
    – 26 rooks
Gadabout, passage falcon – 3 rooks
Score
79 rooks
[Here Endeth]
Total Score

Rooks	5,534
Crows	101
Magpies	422
Rabbits	913
Patridges	1,673
Grouse	1,201
Various	455
Total	10,299 head

As can be seen from the preceding
records, some scores are missing
from the above total.

Glossary

Bate   To flutter off the perch or fist through wildness or anger

Bell   A trained hawk normally wears bells attached to her legs to enable the falconer to find her

Bind   To catch hold of the quarry

Block   The perch used for long-winged hawks when put out to 'weather' on the lawn

Blue hawk   A hawk, more particularly a peregrine, in adult plumage

Bolt, to fly at   To fly straight from the fist at quarry

Bowse   To drink. A hawk is said to bowse when she sips water

Brail   A strip of leather used to secure the wing of a restless hawk

Cadge, or cage   Oblong frame on which hawks are carried to the field

Cast   A cast of hawks, two hawks flown together

Crabbing   (i.e. grabbing) said of a hawk that seizes another

Enter   To fly a hawk at quarry for the first time

Eyas(s)   A nestling or young hawk

Eyrie   The nest of a hawk

Falcon   The female peregrine; also used for the female of other long-winged hawks

Flush   To spring the quarry

Hack, flying at   A state of liberty for eyas hawks, which are kept at liberty and regularly fed at the hack place until able to kill

Haggard   A hawk caught in 'blue' or adult plumage

Hood   A leather cap, used to blindfold a hawk, easily removed or replaced

Imp   To repair a broken feather

Intermewed   A hawk is intermewed when moulted in captivity

Jack   A male merlin

Jerkin   A male gyrfalcon

Jesses   Short leather straps, fastened to a hawk's legs.

Make hawk   An experienced hawk flown in a cast with another to encourage it at quarry

Mews   The hawk house

Musket   A male sparrowhawk

Passage   Regular flight of birds to or from breeding grounds; *also* the annual migration of hawks

Passage hawk   A wild caught hawk in 'red' or immature plumage

Rake   To rake or strike quarry

Red hawk   A hawk in immature, first-year plumage

Ring up   To rise spirally to gain height

Saker   A desert falcon

Slight falcon   Another name for a peregrine

Stoop   To dive or swoop at quarry

Tiercel   A male peregrine; sometimes used of the male goshawk

Wait on   A hawk is said to wait on when she circles over the falconer or dog, often at a great height, waiting for quarry to be flushed

Weather   To puts hawks out in the open, on the lawn, attached to blocks, to enjoy the weather

Index of Hawks

Index of Hawks

Index of Gentlemen and Professional Falconers